This book
belongs to

_____

...a Woman After
God's Own Heart

A Woman After God's Own Heart®

Elizabeth George

HARVEST HOUSE PUBLISHERS

EUGENE, OREGON

A WOMAN AFTER GOD'S OWN HEART*
Copyright © 1997/2006 by Harvest House Publishers
Eugene, Oregon 97402
www.harvesthousepublishers.com

Library of Congress Cataloging-in-Publication Data
George, Elizabeth, 1944– . A woman after God's own heart / Elizabeth George.
    p. cm.

Trade Edition	Deluxe Edition
ISBN: 978-0-7369-1883-1	ISBN: 978-0-7369-2046-9

1. Women—Prayer-books and devotions—English.   2. Christian women—Religious life.
3. Women—Conduct of life. I. Title.
BV4844.G43 1997 96–45436
248.8'43—dc21

Printed in the United States of America

09 10 11 12 13 14 / BP-MS / 10 9 8

To my cherished friends and daughters
Katherine George Zaengle and Courtney George Seitz,
who share my deep desire to become
women after God's own heart.

Acknowledgment

As always, thank you to my dear husband, Jim George, M.Div., Th.M., for your able assistance, guidance, suggestions, and loving encouragement on this project.

Contents

Dear Seeker of God's Heart

God knows how deeply humbled I am each time someone like you writes to let me know how He has used His truths in *A Woman After God's Own Heart®* to positively impact you, your family, your home, and your love for Him. His truths are truly transforming (John 17:17)! And He also knows how blessed I am when someone like you brings a tattered and torn, dirt-darkened, tearstained, coffee-splattered, dog-eared, doodled-on-by-your-children book through a line for me to autograph. As I always say, "The best book is a used book!"

Well, my dear reading friend, at last—thanks to Harvest House Publishers—this wonderful updated and expanded edition of *A Woman After God's Own Heart®* is now available! Its debut was prompted by women like you who have heard me speak from the book or studied through my video Bible study of *A Woman After God's Own Heart*®.[1] These women asked about the additional insights I now share in person or on CD that reflect my growth and understanding of practicing God's priorities for the ten years that have passed since I wrote this book. This new edition is just for you...to read and reread, to carry with your Bible, to take along in your backpack (or diaper bag, as the case may be!), to study with friends, to leave on your nightstand as a refresher, and to bless and encourage others as a life-changing gift.

It's wonderful being a woman after God's own heart, isn't it! To know Him. To love Him. To enrich the lives of others. To follow Him...and to partake of the blessings He extends to us when we do. No woman's life could be more satisfying than the life enjoyed by a woman after His own heart, a woman whose heart's desire is to do God's will (Acts 13:22)! May God richly bless you and yours as you continue to follow after Him.

In His everlasting love,

Elizabeth George

A Word of Welcome

Imagine living life so that people thought of each of us—today and long after we're gone—as a woman after God's own heart!

Thousands of years after he walked this earth, we still think of King David—the faithful shepherd boy who slew Goliath, the warrior who mercifully spared King Saul's life on more than one occasion, the King who danced with joy as the Ark of the Covenant was returned to Jerusalem—as *a man after God's own heart* (1 Samuel 13:14 and Acts 13:22)!

Before you protest, "But I'm hardly in King David's category!" let me remind you that he was far from perfect. (For instance, does the name "Bathsheba" ring a bell?) Despite his tendency to forget to consult God, despite his cold-blooded arrangements to murder Uriah so he could marry Bathsheba, and despite his less than solid parenting, David has been given the title "man after God's own heart." I find that very encouraging as I continue on the path of being a woman after God's own heart.

I also find encouraging the fact that this path is, in the words of Richard Foster, "the path of disciplined Grace."[1] He goes on to explain:

> It is discipline, because there is work for us to do. It is Grace, because the life of God which we enter into is a gift which we can never earn....Discipline in and of itself does not make us righteous, it merely places us before God....The transformation...is God's work.[2]

Our transformation into being a woman after God's own heart is indeed God's work. But what I offer here are the disciplines we can follow to place ourselves before God—disciplines regarding our devotional life, our personal growth, our home, our marriage and family, and our ministry—so that He can do that work in our heart. You'll find practical insights about what it means to follow God in every area of life, insights about nurturing an impassioned relationship with God, experiencing personal growth, caring for your home, loving your husband, enjoying your children, and giving to others. The journey is an exciting one, and you'll find much joy along the way. So I welcome you to join me as each of us seeks to be the woman God calls us...and will empower us...to be, a woman after His own heart.

Part 1

The Pursuit of God

1

A Heart Devoted to God

But one thing is needed, and Mary has chosen that good part,
which will not be taken away from her.
LUKE 10:42

I had done it thousands of times before, but two days ago it was different. I'm talking about the walk I take each day in the dewy part of the morning. As I moved through my neighborhood I noticed a woman—probably in her late seventies—walking on the sidewalk by the park. She had an aluminum walker and appeared to have suffered a stroke. She was also a little bent over, a telltale sign of osteoporosis.

What made this outing different for me? Well, just three days earlier we had buried my husband's mother. Lois was in her late seventies when God called her home to be with Him…and Lois had used an aluminum walker…and Lois had suffered from osteoporosis…and Lois too had experienced a slight stroke.

Still grieving over our recent loss, I was a little down even before

I spotted this woman who so reminded me of Lois. I had already used the few tissues I had taken with me. And my heart and mind were filled with thoughts like *What will we do for Thanksgiving? We always had Thanksgiving at Lois's. She always fixed the turkey, dressing, cranberry sauce, and homemade pies. What will a family gathering be like without her?* On and on my thoughts went. *She won't be in her regular seat at church Sunday....I no longer have any reason to take the freeway exit that leads to her house. Besides, it is no longer her house....Now who was praying for us? How will the loss of her prayer power affect all of us—Jim's ministry, my ministry, the girls' lives, this book?*

As I watched that dear, brave woman struggling to walk and remembered Lois's battle with cancer and pneumonia at the end of her life, I realized I was taking a hard look at reality. Every one of us has a body that will someday fail us—and that someday is not necessarily too far off.

I was also sharply reminded once again of how desperately I want my life—indeed each and every day of it, each and every minute of it—to count. Yet as I took in this scene and thought these thoughts, I was aware that my fiftieth birthday had come—and gone. My thirtieth wedding anniversary had done the same. And my two little babies had graduated from life at home to life in their own homes with husbands to love and babies of their own to consider. I was running out of time!

A Change of Heart

Now I don't want you to think this book is a "downer"! This is certainly not at all how I intended to begin a book about a woman after God's own heart. But these thoughts don't mark the end of my walk—or my story. Let me tell you what happened next.

As I pushed forward on my walk, I realized that I needed to push

my thoughts forward too. I had been thinking earthly thoughts—
human thoughts, physical thoughts, worldly thoughts—rather
than thoughts of faith. My perspective was off! We as Christians
are to walk by faith, not by sight (2 Corinthians 5:7), so I turned
my mind and heart upward and began to adjust my perspective
to match God's view of my life (and Lois's life and yours), His
eternal view that encompasses our past and our future as well as
our present.

Rushing to my rescue was one particular verse from the Bible.
I had memorized it long ago and had since applied it to my life in
many ways. The words were fresh in my mind because the pastor
who had shared the platform with my husband, Jim (Lois's son
and only child), at her memorial service had used it when speaking of her life. They were words Jesus had spoken of to Mary, the
sister of Lazarus and Martha. He said, "But one thing is needed,
and Mary has chosen that good part, which will not be taken
away from her" (Luke 10:42).

As I thought on this word from God about one of His
women—a woman Jesus was
defending from criticism with
this statement—I found myself
looking straight into the core
meaning of "a heart after God,"
and I was greatly comforted.

> *To be God's women,*
> *to love Him fervently*
> *with whole hearts, is*
> *our sole desire.*

First, I was comforted about
Lois. Although her life with us was over, she had sought to make
it count every day and for eternity. She had chosen the one thing,
the necessary thing, each day for most of her life. She had chosen
with her whole heart to seek to live her life for God. She loved
God, worshiped God, walked with God, served God, and looked
forward to being with Him in eternity. In spite of a painful cancer

and being twice widowed, Lois knew true inner peace and joy as she nurtured a heart of devotion to God. I have no doubt that my mother-in-law's life had definitely counted for the kingdom.

I was also comforted about my own life. After all, God knows the desires of my heart—indeed, He has put them there (Psalm 37:4)! He knows the amount of daydreaming—and praying—I do about becoming the kind of woman He wants me to be. He also knows that while I am daydreaming I am frightfully aware that the years are drifting by and that there is less and less time left for becoming that woman. But God's peace became mine as I was reminded one more time that when, day by day, I choose the one thing necessary—which shall never be taken away from me—my life too makes a difference. God wants my heart—all of it—and my devotion. When I choose to give it to Him, when I choose to live totally for Him, He makes it count. He wants to be Number One in my life, the priority above all priorities!

And, dear friend and woman after God's heart, I am comforted for you too because I know you join me in yearning for the things of God. To be God's woman, to love Him fervently with a whole heart, is our sole desire. And whether you're pushing a stroller or a grocery cart or an aluminum walker, whether you're single, married, or a widow, whether your challenge is eight children or no children, whether life has you nursing children with measles, a husband with cancer, or your own osteoporosis, your life counts—and counts mightily—as you face its challenges with a heart full of devotion to God.

As I said earlier, I had not planned to open this book with thoughts like these. But because of the life Lois nurtured and chose each day to live, a tribute to her is a fitting beginning for a book about a woman after God's own heart. Lois showed me how important it is to choose to love God and follow after Him…with a whole heart…each day…as long as we live. Every day counts when we are devoted to God!

A Heart Devoted to God

A closer look at Mary, a woman who sat at Jesus' feet and received His praise, further opens up for us the meaning of a heart devoted to God. What did Mary do that moved our Savior to praise her?

Mary discerned the one thing needed—The events leading up to Jesus' words set the scene for us to look into Mary's heart (Luke 10:38-42). Jesus (probably accompanied by His disciples) arrived at the home of Mary's sister, Martha, for a meal. I'm sure it was a joyous and festive time. Imagine, God in flesh coming for dinner! He was total love, total care, total concern, and total wisdom. It would be heaven on earth to be in His presence— the presence of God.

But Martha, Mary's sister, didn't discern the miracle of God in the flesh. Consequently, she marred His visit by her behavior. She crossed over the line of graciously providing food and became overly involved in her hostessing. When Jesus opened His mouth to impart words of life—the Word of God spoken by God Himself—and Mary slipped out of the kitchen to sit quietly at His feet, Martha broke. She interrupted the Teacher, her guest, to say something to this effect—"Don't you care that I'm putting this meal together all by myself? Tell Mary to help me!" Martha failed to discern the priority and importance of time with God.

Mary, a woman after God's own heart, made the choice that indicated her heart's devotion: She knew it was important to cease her busyness, stop all activity, and set aside secondary things in order to focus wholly on the Lord. Unlike her sister, who was so busy doing things *for* the Lord that she failed to spend time *with* Him, Mary put worship at the top of her to-do list.

Mary chose the one thing needed—Because Mary was a woman after God's own heart, she was preoccupied with one thing at all times—Him! Yes, she too served. And she too tried to fulfill her God-given responsibilities. But there was one choice that Mary made that day in Bethany, a decision to do the one thing that mattered most: Mary chose to spend time worshiping God. She knew that nothing can take the place of time in God's presence. Indeed, time spent sitting at His feet fuels and focuses all acts of service. And, as her Master noted, time spent hearing and worshiping God can never be taken away, for it is time spent in eternal pursuits, time that earns permanent and everlasting dividends. Mary chose to spend that precious time with Him.

Yes, But How?

How can you and I become women devoted to God, women who love God deeply and live for Him daily? What can we do to follow Mary's example and begin making choices that tell the whole watching world that we are women after God's own heart, choices that position us so God can impassion our hearts toward Him?

1. *Choose God's ways at every opportunity*—Commit yourself to actively choose God and His ways—as Mary did—in your decisions, words, thoughts, and responses. *A Woman After God's Own Heart* is about living according to God's priorities, and we want the choices we make to reflect that God is our Ultimate Priority. After all, the word "priority" means "to prefer." We want to choose to prefer God's way in all things. And several guidelines

help. This is simple but, believe me, I know how easy it is to let our guard down.

Proverbs 3:6—"In all your ways acknowledge Him, and He shall direct your paths" could be the theme verse of this book—and of life! This well-loved verse describes a two-step partnership with God. Our part is to stop and acknowledge God along the way, and His part is to direct our paths. This means we are to consult with God regarding our decisions, thoughts, words spoken, or responses. Before we move ahead or merely react, we need to stop and pray first, "God, what would You have me do—or think or say—here?"

What exactly does Proverbs 3:6 look like in daily life? Let me share two examples. I wake up and the day begins. As I merrily go about the business of life, a crisis suddenly arises. The phone rings, and it's bad news or a decision needs to be made. I try to remember to mentally—and maybe even physically (as Mary did)—stop and check in with God. I pray, "God, what do You want me to do here?" I endeavor to simply pause in my mind and spirit and acknowledge God. That's my part of the partnership. It may take a split second or some minutes in prayer.

Or I'm again merrily going about my day—and I run into someone who says something that hurts me. Before I blurt something out (this is my goal anyway!), before I give an eye for an eye (or a word for a word), I try again to stop...pause...sit mentally in God's presence...and lift my thoughts to Him: "O.K., God, what do You want me to do here? What do You want me to say? How do You want me to act?" I even ask Him, "What expression do You want on my face as I listen to this person say these things?" I acknowledge God. That's my part.

And then God takes over and does His part—He directs my

paths. Often it's almost as if the next thought to enter my mind is from Him. Because I ask Him for direction and want to do things His way—not my way—He directs me. He instructs me and teaches me in the way I should go (Psalm 32:8). He guides me in what to do, how to act, and what to say. God is faithful to His promise: "Your ears shall hear a word behind you, saying, 'This is the way, walk in it'" (Isaiah 30:21).

The saying "good, better, best"—Perhaps as a child you heard your teacher at school say,

> Good, better, best,
> never let it rest,
> until your good is better,
> and your better best.

Well, I try to apply this saying in very practical ways to my own decision-making and choices. That's what Mary did. According to Jesus, she chose the *best* way. Here's just one way that doing so has helped me.

Choosing God and His ways deepens our devotion to Him.

In Los Angeles people can spend a lot of time in the car, and I was no exception. There in the car—all alone—I had options about what I could think and do. For years I drove around with an easy-listening music station on the radio. That was a fairly good choice. However, after some thought, I decided a better choice for me would be to listen to classical music (a passion of mine). After thinking about my choice a little more, I decided an even better choice would be playing a CD of uplifting Christian music. Then I moved up the "better" scale again as I chose to listen to sermon CDs instead—recordings of a man of God teaching the Word of God to the people of God. Next, playing CDs of the Bible seemed even better. Then one day I turned the whole audio system off and landed on what for me was the best choice for my car time—memorizing Scripture. Good to better to best!

When I was a new Christian, I heard a more spiritually mature woman at church tell about a choice—a Mary kind of choice— she made each day as soon as her husband left for work. She said she could do almost anything she wanted—turn on the TV and watch a soap opera or talk show, read the *Los Angeles Times,* or— her choice—pick up her Bible and have her quiet time. Here was a woman—a woman after God's own heart—paying close attention to what was good, better, and best, and striving to make the best choices.

That, dear reader, is our challenge too. Choosing God and His ways deepens our devotion to Him.

Standing in awe of God—A favorite passage of mine ends with these words: "Charm is deceitful and beauty is passing, but *a woman who fears the LORD,* she shall be praised" (Proverbs 31:30).

Author and Bible teacher Anne Ortlund expressed her own awe of God: "In my heart I do have a fear....I long to grow more godly with each passing day. Call it 'the fear of the Lord,' being in awe of Him and scared to death of any sin that would mar my life at this point."[1]

This same heart for God and fear of missing His best because of faulty choices was shared by another woman I admire, Carole Mayhall of the Christian discipleship organization The Navigators. Twice I've heard Carole share at women's retreats, and both times she said, "Daily I live with [one] fear—a healthy fear if there is

such a thing. [It is] that I will miss something God has for me
in this life. And it is mind-expanding to contemplate all that
He wants me to have. I don't want to be robbed of even one of
God's riches by not taking time to let Him invade my life. By
not listening to what He is telling me. By allowing the routine,
pressing matters of my minutes to bankrupt me of time for the
most exciting, most fulfilling relationship in life."[2]

Are you in awe of God and what He wants to do in you, for
you, and through you?

2. *Commit yourself to God daily*—Our devotion to God is
strengthened when we offer Him a fresh commitment each day.
Every morning, in a heartfelt prayer either written or silent, start
fresh with God by giving Him all that you are, all that you have...
now...forever...and daily. Lay everything on God's altar in what
one saint of old called the "surrendered life."[3] Give God your life,
your body (such as it is), your health (or lack of it), your husband,
each child (one by one), your home, your possessions. Nurture
the habit of placing these blessings in God's loving hands to do
with them what He will. After all, they are not ours—they are
His! A daily prayer of commitment helps us to release what we
think are our rights to these gifts. As the saying goes, "Hold all
things lightly and nothing tightly." I also find these words from
nineteenth-century devotional writer Andrew Murray helpful:
"God is ready to assume full responsibility for the life wholly
yielded to Him."[4]

So aim at some kind of commitment to God made daily. It
can be as simple as this prayer, the first of F.B. Meyer's seven rules
for living: "Make a daily, definite, audible consecration of yourself to God. Say it out loud: 'Lord, today I give myself anew to
you.'"[5]

Perhaps the prayer of commitment I love best (and have written on the front page of my Bible) is that of Betty Scott Stam, a China Inland Mission worker. She and her husband were led through the streets of China to their execution by decapitation, while their baby lay behind in its crib. This was her daily prayer:

> Lord, I give up all my own plans and purposes,
> all my own desires and hopes, and accept Thy will
> for my life. I give myself, my time, my all, utterly to
> Thee to be Thine forever. Fill me and seal me with
> Thy Holy Spirit. Use me as Thou wilt, send me
> where Thou wilt, work out Thy whole will in my
> life at any cost, now and forever.[6]

In this case, the cost was high. This total commitment to God cost Betty Stam her ministry, her husband, her child, her life. But that kind of commitment is indeed our high calling as His children (Romans 8:17).

3. *Cultivate a hot heart*—I am especially challenged about the temperature of my own heart whenever I consider these words spoken by Jesus: "I know your works, that you are neither cold nor hot. I could wish you were cold or hot. So then, because you are lukewarm, and neither cold nor hot, I will vomit you out of My mouth" (Revelation 3:15-16). According to this Scripture, which heart condition do you think God considers the worst?

Think about these chilling facts: To be cold-hearted means to be decidedly below normal, to be unemotional, unaware, unconscious of God. Imagine…being unemotional about the things of God! And then there's the lukewarm heart. It's only moderately warm. It's indifferent! Imagine being indifferent toward God!

Hot—the third option—is where we want to be. That's having

> *We should be fiery and excited about God, and God will fuel our fire.*

a high temperature, characterized by violent activity, emotion, or passion. It's fiery and excited. Now that's the heart of someone committed to God!

Have you ever been in the presence of a person who is hot-hearted toward God? I have. Mike was asked to say grace at a potluck dinner. Well, when you have a hot heart for God you can never just say grace. Prostrate in his heart and soul, Mike began a prayer of heartfelt worship. His passion tumbled out of his mouth as he thanked God for His salvation, for the fact that he had been transferred from darkness into the kingdom of light, that he had been lost but was now found, blind but could now see. On and on Mike went until I, frankly, lost my appetite because I had found other meat—for the soul! Mike's hot heart moved me to forget about a mere hot meal for my stomach.

Our heart for God should be like a boiling pot. Our heart should be characterized by God-given and intense passion for our Lord. After all, when a teakettle is boiling on your stove, you know it. It sputters and steams. It actually hops up and down and jiggles from side to side, empowered by its violent heat. Hot to the touch, it shares the heat that is within. There is no way to ignore its fire. Likewise, we should be fiery and excited about God, and God will fuel our fire.

That's what I want for you—and for myself. I want Jesus' presence in our lives to make a difference. I want us to overflow with His goodness and praise. I want our lips to speak of the great things He has done for us (Luke 1:49), to tell of His wonders (Psalm 96:3). "Let the redeemed of the LORD say so" (Psalm 107:2)!

Heart Response

Oh, dear sister, how would you rate your heart condition? I pray that your heart belongs to Christ, that you have entered into an eternal relationship with God through His Son, Jesus. If this is true for you, thank Him for the wonderful privilege of being called a child of God!

However, if you are unsure about where you stand with God or if you know quite clearly you are living your life apart from God, purpose to make things right with Him. Spend time in prayer. Confess and deal with any sin. Invite Jesus to be your Savior, and by doing so, welcome Christ into your life and become a new creature in Him (2 Corinthians 5:17). Your prayer might go something like this:

> God, I want to be Your child, a true woman after Your heart—a woman who lives her life in You, through You, and for You. I acknowledge my sin and receive Your Son, Jesus Christ, into my needy heart, giving thanks that He died on the cross for my sins. Thank You for giving me Your strength so that I can follow after Your heart.

Go ahead. Turn your heart heavenward. Open up your heart. Invite Christ in. He will then make you a woman after His own heart!

Now you can begin—or begin anew!—to put yourself in a position where God can grow in you a heart of devotion. Every activity in this book is aimed at helping you place yourself before God so He can turn your heart toward Him. Our goal is to have no will but His will. Right now utter a prayer for more heat!

2

A Heart Abiding in God's Word

For [you] shall be like a tree planted by the waters,
which spreads out its roots by the river.
JEREMIAH 17:8

The Bible speaks of "a time to plant" (Ecclesiastes 3:2), and for my husband, Jim, that time came as a result of the massive 1994 earthquake we went through in Southern California. A part of the devastation we experienced at our home (only three miles from the quake's epicenter) was the loss of our block-wall fences.

After a year of waving to our neighbors only a few feet away, it was a blessing to have those fences back in place. But the new walls were so bleak. So naked. The old ones had been charming—seasoned by age, blanketed by climbing roses and ivy, serving as friendly arms that embraced our lawn, patio, house, and anyone who happened to be there enjoying the beauty. Its stark-but-hidden stone facade had functioned as an invisible support for far lovelier things—things alive and blooming that added fragrance, color, and ambiance to our yard. And now we were forced to start all over again. It was our time to plant.

So Jim planted…13 baby creeping figs whose job was to soften the harshness of the new walls. Twelve of those new figs dutifully shot out their magic fingers and began a friendly possession of the wall. One plant, however, slowly withered, shrank, and finally died.

Coming home from work on a Friday afternoon, Jim picked up a replacement plant at the nursery, changed clothes, got out our shovel, and bent over the dead vine, fully prepared to work at digging it out of the ground so he could put the new one in. But, much to his surprise, the shovel wasn't necessary. As he grasped the plant, it easily came out of the ground. There were no roots! Although the plant had enjoyed all the right conditions above ground, something was missing beneath the surface of the soil. It didn't have the root system vital for drawing the needed nourishment and moisture from the soil.

This garden scenario portrays a spiritual truth for you and me as God grows in us a heart of faith: We must nurture a root system! Roots make all the difference in the health of a plant, and their presence or absence ultimately becomes known to all. The plant either flourishes or fails, thrives or dies, blossoms or withers. The health of anything—whether a garden plant or a heart devoted to God—reflects what is going on (or not going on!) underground.

Drawing Life from God's Word

If God is going to be first in our hearts and the "Ultimate Priority" of our lives, we must develop a root system anchored deep in Him. Just like a plant with its roots hidden underground, you and I—out of public view and alone with God—are to draw from Him all that we need to live the abundant life He has promised His children (John 10:10). We must seek to live our lives near to God—indeed, hidden in Him! As we seek a deeper life in Christ, we do well to consider some facts about roots.

Roots are unseen—Like a creeping fig or any other plant, your spiritual roots are underground, invisible to others. I'm talking about your private life, your hidden life, the secret life you enjoy with God out of the public eye. An iceberg illustrates the importance of what is hidden.

When Jim and I were teaching in Alaska, a commercial fisherman took Jim out on his boat. Not only did Jeff show Jim eagles, seals, and whales, but Jeff also gingerly guided his boat around an iceberg. He explained to Jim that only one-seventh of an iceberg is visible above the surface, and any wise fisherman knows not to get too close because underneath spreads the other six-sevenths. What was visible to the eye—only a fraction of the huge, icy mass—was enough to evoke fear, awe, and respect in any sailor.

And that's what you and I want for our lives. We want what other people see of our lives—the public portion—to stir up this kind of awe and wonder. We want our strength in public to be explained by what goes on in private between us and God.

But it's so easy for you and me to get this all backwards. It's easy to think that what counts in the Christian life is the time spent in public with people, people, and more people. We seem to always be with people—people at work, people on campus, people in the dorms, people from Bible studies, people we live with, people in discipleship settings or fellowship groups.

> *The impact of your ministry to people will be in direct proportion to the time you spend with God.*

But the truth is that "the greater the proportion of your day—of your life—spent hidden in quiet, in reflection, in prayer, [in study,] in scheduling, in preparation, the greater will be the effectiveness, the impact, the power, of the part of your life that shows."[1] As I heard one Christian leader say, you cannot be *with* people all of the time and have a ministry *to* people. The impact of your ministry to people will be in direct proportion to the time you spend away from people and with God.

And our effectiveness for the Lord requires wise decisions regarding time. I carry in my Bible a quote that helps me make the kinds of choices that allow time for developing the underground life: "We [must] say 'no' not only to things which are wrong and sinful, but to things pleasant, profitable, and good which would hinder and clog our grand duties and our chief work."[2] (What are those "pleasant, profitable, and good things" for you?)

Our effectiveness for the Lord also requires solitude. In his little book *The Greatest Thing in the World*, Henry Drummond made this observation: "Talent develops itself in solitude; the talent of prayer, of faith, of meditation, of seeing the unseen."[3] So that our roots grow deep into Him, God calls us away from this world.

Roots are for taking in—What happens when you and I do slip away to be with God in study and prayer? We receive. We take in. We are nurtured and fed. We ensure our spiritual health and growth. When we spend time with Christ, He supplies us with strength and encourages us in the pursuit of His ways.

I call this time with God "the great exchange." Away from the world and hidden from public view, I exchange my weariness for His strength, my weakness for His power, my darkness for His light, my problems for His solutions, my burdens for

His freedom, my frustrations for His peace, my turmoil for His calm, my hopes for His promises, my afflictions for His balm of comfort, my questions for His answers, my confusion for His knowledge, my doubt for His assurance, my nothingness for His awesomeness, the temporal for the eternal, and the impossible for the possible.

I saw the reality of this great exchange at one of our church's annual women's retreats. My roommate and dear friend was in charge of this event, which was attended by approximately 500 women. Karen handled each challenge graciously and put her administrative genius to work with each crisis. But I noticed that as the starting time for each session neared and panic rose among the organizers who hoped things would go smoothly, Karen disappeared. As breathless, perspiring, frazzled women came running into our room asking, "Where's Karen? We've got a problem!" she was nowhere to be found.

On one of those mysterious occasions, I glimpsed Karen walking down the hotel hall with her retreat folder and burgundy Bible in hand. She had prepared well in advance for the approaching session. She had carefully gone over the plans, the schedule, and the announcements one last time. But she sensed a need for one more thing—quiet time with God alone. She needed to look at a few precious portions of His empowering Word and then place our event completely in His hands through prayer.

Later—after Karen reappeared from her time of taking in— I couldn't help but notice the sharp contrast between her and the others. As the anxiety of other women rose, Karen exhibited God's perfect peace. As they fretted, worried, and wondered, Karen knew all was and would be well. As others wilted under the pressure, Karen's strength—God's strength in Karen—shone with supernatural brilliance. Underground and away from the crowd, she had exchanged her needs for God's supply.

Roots are for storage—Roots serve as a reservoir of what we need. Jeremiah 17 tells us that the person who trusts in the Lord...

> shall be like a tree planted by the waters,
> which spreads out its roots by the river,
> and will not fear when heat comes;
> but its leaf will be green,
> and will not be anxious in the year of drought,
> nor will cease from yielding fruit (verse 8).

This trusting soul, whose roots are collecting life-giving water, will exhibit several qualities.

First, she will *not be afraid* of the scorching heat, even if the days turn into a long year of drought. Instead she will endure the heat with leaves of green. The reservoir she has stored up from God's Word will sustain her through the fiery trials, no matter how long they last.

She will also *bear fruit faithfully*. She will not cease to yield fruit even in times of drought. Because of stored-up nourishment from God Himself, she will be like a tree of life—producing in and sometimes even out of season (Psalm 1:3).

As you and I regularly draw needed refreshment from God's Word, He creates in us a reservoir of hope and strength in Him. Then, when times are rough, we won't be depleted. We won't dry up, disintegrate, or die. We won't run out of gas, collapse, exhaust, or give out. Instead we will simply reach down into our

> *Roots deep into God's truth are definitely needed as reserves when times are rough.*

hidden reservoir of refreshment and draw out what we need right now from what God has given us. We will be able to go from "strength to strength" (Psalm 84:7).

This is exactly what happened to me during my mother-in-law's illness. Her hospitalization was a crisis that challenged my endurance. My husband—her only child—was overseas and literally unreachable. Because of the constant demands of this difficult season, I had no chance for formal quiet times. As I stood by Lois's bed, tending to her by the hour, I had no option but to reach down into my reservoir.

And what did I find stored up there? As evidence of God's marvelous grace, I found strength in many Scriptures I had memorized over the years. I gained spiritual energy from psalms read, studied, and prayed through in earlier (and quieter) times alone with God. As I tapped into God's power through prayer, I experienced His peace that passes all understanding guarding my heart (Philippians 4:7). And I was fortified by the example of my Savior and a host of men and women in the Bible who had also drawn what they needed from God's Word. Roots deep into God's truth are definitely needed as reserves when times are rough!

Roots are for support—Without a well-developed root system, we become top heavy—lots of leafy, heavy foliage appears above ground but nothing supports it from underneath. Without a network of strong roots, sooner or later we have to be staked up, tied up, propped up, straightened up—until the next wind comes along and we fall over again. But with firm, healthy roots, no wind can blow us down.

Yes, the support of a healthy root system is vital for standing strong in the Lord! I'm reminded of the process used in bygone days for growing the trees that became the main masts for military

and merchant ships. The great shipbuilders first selected a tree
located on the top of a high hill as a potential mast. Then they
cut away all of the surrounding trees that would shield the chosen
one from the force of the wind. As the years went by and the
winds blew fiercely against the tree, the tree grew stronger until
finally it was strong enough to be the foremast of a ship.[4] When
we have a solid root system, we too can gain the strength needed
for standing firm in spite of the pressures of life!

Yes, But How?

How does a woman draw near to God's heart? What can we
do to put ourselves in a position where God can grow each of us
into a woman of remarkable endurance?

1. *Develop the habit of drawing near to God*—Only through
routine, regular exposure to God's Word can you and I draw out
the nutrition needed to grow hearts of faith. I know firsthand
how hard it is to develop the habit of drawing near to God and
how easy it is to skip and miss. For some reason I tend to think I'll
spend time with God later, I'll get around to it in a little while, or
I'll miss just this one day—but catch up with God tomorrow.

I've learned, however, that my good intentions don't go very
far. It's easy for me to start the day planning to have a devotional time a little later...after I've done a few things around the
house, made some phone calls, tidied up the kitchen, started the
dishwasher, made the bed, and picked up those clothes on the
floor, and—oh, I almost forgot—wiped off the bathroom counter. Suddenly I'm off and running. Somehow I never get to time
for the most important relationship in my life—my relationship
with God! That's why I have to be firm with myself and aim for
habitual, scheduled time with God whether I *feel* like it or not,

whether it *seems* like the best use of my time or not. I must draw near to God.

Here's a question to think about: If someone asked you to describe the quiet time you had this morning, what would you say? This is exactly the question Dawson Trotman, founder of The Navigators ministry organization, asked men and women applying for missions work. He once spent five days interviewing candidates for overseas missionary service. He spent a half hour with each one, asking specifically about their devotional life. Sadly, only one person out of 29 interviewed said his devotional life was a constant in his life, a source of strength, guidance, and refreshment. As Trotman continued to probe into the lives of those men and women planning a lifetime of service for God, he found that since they had come to know the Lord, they had never had a consistent devotional life![5]

Developing the habit of drawing near to God definitely helps make our devotional life what we need it to be—and what God wants it to be! To help make this a reality, I've placed a "Quiet Times Calendar" at the back of this book just for you. As you use it, aim for consistency. Begin with even a brief time each day. Great lives are made up of many "little" disciplines. Begin the "little" discipline of meeting with the Lord daily and then filling in your Quiet Times Calendar. Just fill in the squares for each day that you have a quiet time. Remember that the goal is solid lines—like a thermometer, not a "Morse code" measurement (dot-dot-dash) or a "measles" measurement (here a dot, there a dot, everywhere a dot dot). I pray you'll be blessed like this dear woman was:

I have been attempting to have daily quiet times
for awhile now. This past week, however, I found

that having to actually record the days I had my quiet time has encouraged me to be more faithful with them. Instead of brushing it aside in the morning, I chose to have it, even if it couldn't be as long as I hoped for.

2. *Design a personal time for drawing near to God*—As women we're used to designing, planning, and scheduling the events of life. We know how to pull off parties, projects at work, weddings, and retreats. When it comes to planning, your quiet time should be no different—especially considering its eternal value. Consider what kind of quiet time would be ideal for you. What elements would make it a quality time?

When? Keep in mind one of my mottos: *Something is better than nothing.* The only "wrong" time for having your time alone with God would be *no* time. So pick a time that matches your lifestyle. Some moms of newborns have their time with the Lord in the middle of the night when they are awakened by a crying baby. Some working women have theirs during the lunch break— in the car, in a restaurant, or at their desks. My dear mother-in-law had hers at night in bed because pain made sleep difficult, and God's Word helped her relax and rest. Another woman takes her calendar in hand every Sunday afternoon, looks at the week's events, and then makes an appointment with God at the time that best fits each day. Hudson Taylor admitted to a friend that "the sun has never risen upon China without finding me at prayer."[6] How did he accomplish that? "To ensure a quiet time for uninterrupted prayer, he always rose very early in the morning before daylight and, if nature demanded it, would continue his sleep after his season of prayer."[7] When would be best for *you?* Once you pinpoint the best time, you've taken an important first step!

Where? Right now my bed is my place, but for many years I used the breakfast table. Then, for some reason, I moved into the living room and took over the couch and coffee table. In the summer the patio is my spot. It doesn't matter where you meet the Lord—as long as you do it! I have friends who set up desks and counters as their place to be alone with God. Another woman converted an antique cupboard to meet her needs. A book I read suggested purchasing a door at the hardware store and laying it across two low file cabinets.[8] Another woman converted a hall closet into her "prayer closet." Do what you need to do to make a specific spot *your* place to meet with the Lord.

What aids? Gather some essentials—a good reading light, highlighters, pens, pencils, markers, sticky notes, 3" x 5" cards, legal pads for writing, a prayer notebook, and a box of tissues. You might add a hymnal to guide your singing or a CD player for Christian praise or teaching CDs. Maybe you need your memory verses, a journal, a Bible-reading schedule, a devotional book, or some reference books. Whatever you need, see that it's there.

Whatever it takes, fellow seeker after God's heart, do what you must to be alone with God so that He can fine-tune your heart to His. As one wise saint wrote, "Every believer may and must have his time when he is indeed himself alone with God. Oh, the thought to have God all alone to myself, and to know that God has me all alone to Himself!"[9]

3. *Dream of being a woman after God's heart!*—Motivation is key when it comes to nurturing a heart of devotion, and dreaming helps motivate us. As a wake-up call to the seriousness of daily life and to find fresh urgency about your walk with the Lord, *describe the woman you want to be spiritually in one year.* Let your answer put wings on your dreams.

> *God will take you as far as you want to go, as fast as you want to go.*

Do you realize that in one year you could attack a weak area in your Christian life and gain the victory? You could read through the entire Bible. You could be ready for the mission field. You could be mentored by an older woman—or mentor a younger one yourself (Titus 2:3-5). You could complete a counseling training curriculum or some training in evangelism. You could finish a one-year Bible school course. You could memorize xx verses from the Bible—you choose the number. (After his conversion, Dawson Trotman began to memorize one verse a day for the first three years of his Christian life—that's a thousand verses!)[10] You could read a dozen quality Christian books. Dream on—and do it!

Next, *describe the woman you want to be spiritually ten years from now.* Jot your present age in the margin here and write underneath it the age you will be in ten years. Imagine what those intervening ten years might hold, and you'll see that you will need God for the events of those years! You will need God to help you overcome areas of sin and grow spiritually. You will need Him to help you be a wife...or to be single...or when you become a widow. You will need God to help you be a mother—no matter what the ages of your children. You will need God if you are to be His kind of daughter, daughter-in-law, or mother-in-law. You will need God to help you successfully serve others. You will need God as you care for aging parents. You will need God as you move into old age yourself. And you will need God when you die.

Do you believe you can be this woman? With God's grace and in His strength you can! That's His role in your life. But there is also a place for your effort. As Scripture says, "[*You*] keep your heart with all diligence, for out of it spring the issues of life" (Proverbs 4:23).] You determine some elements of the heart. You decide what you will or will not do, whether you will or will not grow. You also decide the rate at which you will grow—the hit-and-miss rate, the measles rate (a sudden rash here and there), the 5-minute-a-day rate, or the 30-minute-a-day rate. You decide if you want to be a mushroom, which appears for a night and shrivels away at the first hint of wind or heat, or an oak tree, which lasts and lasts and lasts, becoming stronger and mightier with each passing year. As my husband continually challenged his students at The Master's Seminary in years past, "God will take you as far as you want to go, as fast as you want to go." So how far...and how fast...do you want to move toward becoming the woman of your dreams?

Heart Response

Well, here we are—women with hearts after God, dreaming of "more love to Thee, O Christ, more love to Thee!" Here we stand, staring at the very core of God's heart—God's own Word. Truly the treasures of God's Word are fathomless (Romans 11:33). His Word stands as His counsel forever, the thoughts of His heart to all generations (Psalm 33:11). By it we were born again (1 Peter 1:23), by it we grow (1 Peter 2:2), and by it we walk through life as it lights the path for our feet (Psalm 119:105). Surely drawing near to God's Word should be of utmost importance to us each day. What joy we discover when we grow to love it more than food for our bodies (Job 23:12).

At one time I cut out and kept an obituary of a composer who made himself work on his music at least 600 hours each year, keeping track in a diary of each day's progress.[11] He spent his entire life on something good, but something temporal, something with no eternal value. Now imagine what kind of transformation would occur in your heart if you spent time—or more time—drawing near to God through His Word—time spent on something of eternal, life-changing value! Won't you purpose in your heart to spend more time near to God's heart by spending more time in His Word?

3

A Heart Committed to Prayer

I will lift up my eyes to the hills—
from whence comes my help?
My help comes from the LORD.
PSALM 121:1-2

I remember one particularly special day of my life very clearly. It was my tenth spiritual birthday and a significant turning point for me. Having dropped my two daughters off at school and gotten my husband off to work, I sat at my old desk in the family room, alone in the house with only the sound of our wall clock ticking. Resting there before God and rejoicing in a decade of being His child, I thought back over those ten years. Although at times they'd been rough, God's great mercy, His wisdom in every circumstance, and His care in leading and keeping me were all very obvious.

I shuddered at the memories of how my life had been without Him. Overwhelmed by emotion and crying tears of joy, I lifted

my heart in a time of thanksgiving to God. Still with a heart full
of gratitude, I dabbed my eyes, took a deep breath, and prayed,
"Lord, what do You see missing from my Christian life? What
needs attention as I begin a new decade with You?" God seemed
to respond immediately by calling to my mind an area of great
personal struggle and failure—my prayer life.

Oh, I had tried praying. But each new effort lasted, at best,
only a few days. I would set aside time for God, read my Bible,
and then dutifully bow my head, only to mumble a few general
words that basically added up to "God, please bless my family
and me today." Certainly God intended prayer to be more than
that—but I couldn't seem to do it.

But on that tenth spiritual birthday I reached for a small
book of blank pages that my daughter Katherine had given me
for Mother's Day four months earlier. It had sat unused on the
coffee table because I hadn't quite known what to do with it.
But suddenly I knew exactly how to put it to use. Full of resolve,
conviction, and desire, I wrote these words—straight from my
heart—on the first page: "I dedicate and purpose to spend the next
ten years (Lord willing) developing a meaningful prayer life."

These are simple words, written and prayed from a simple
desire within my heart. But that day those simple words and that
little blank book began an exciting leg on my journey and adventure of following after God's own heart! My new commitment to
prayer put into motion a complete makeover of my whole life—
every part and person and pursuit in it.

When I decided to learn more about the awesome privilege of
prayer, I fully expected drudgery and joyless labor. But as I moved
ahead to develop a meaningful prayer life, I was surprised by the
blessings that began to blossom in my heart. As a favorite hymn
tells us, "Count your blessings, name them one by one." I want

to name a few blessings of prayer now because they are blessings that you too can know as you cultivate a heart of prayer.

Blessing #1: A Deeper Relationship with God

Although I'd heard that prayer would deepen my relationship with God, I had never experienced it. But when I started to spend regular, daily, unhurried time in prayer—when I lingered in intimate communion with God—that deeper relationship was mine. When you and I commune in prayer with God, we grow spiritually in a multitude of ways.

Prayer increases faith—I now know firsthand that this is true. I saw it for myself when I followed some advice I once heard. When some parents asked Dr. Howard Hendricks of Dallas Theological Seminary how to teach their children about faith in God, he answered, "Have them keep a prayer list." And that is exactly what I did. Like a child, I wrote out a prayer list in my special book and began taking my concerns to God, my Father, each day. I was awed as, for the first time ever, I paid close attention to how He answered item after item.

Prayer provides a place to unload burdens—Problems and sorrows are facts of life (John 16:33), but I didn't know how to handle them apart from the verse of Scripture that instructed me to cast all my cares and burdens on God (1 Peter 5:7). So, armed with this advice, I rolled up my sleeves and went to work forwarding my concerns to God in prayer. Soon it became natural for me to start each day by giving all the cares of life to God in prayer, and I would rise up relieved, freed from many heavy weights. Author and fellow pray-er Corrie ten Boom offers a vivid image of this privilege:

As a camel kneels before his master to have him
remove his burden, so kneel and let the Master take
your burden.[1]

Prayer teaches us that God is always near—A verse that I recited
thousands of times during the thousands of aftershocks following
the 1994 Northridge earthquake was Psalm 46:1—"God is our
refuge and strength, a *very present help* in trouble." God is always
near, and the more I prayed, the more this truth struck home. I
began to realize the fact of His omnipresence, the reality that He
is always present with His people, including me and you! I found
Oswald Chambers' words to be true: "The purpose of prayer is
to reveal the presence of God equally present all the time in every
condition."[2] Cultivating a heart of prayer is a sure way to experience God's presence.

Prayer trains us not to panic—Jesus taught His disciples that
we ought always to pray and not to faint (Luke 18:1). Turning to
God for every need during my regular daily prayer time ingrained
in me the habit of prayer. Soon I was replacing my tendency to
panic at the first hint of any problem with God's strength—and
I'd make the switch on the spot through prayer!

A Prayer for Peace

Grant that it may not be in the power of any to
rob me of the peace that results from a firm trust in
Thee. Whenever crosses or troubles are met without, may all be well within.[3]

—Susanna Wesley

Prayer changes lives—You've probably heard the saying, "Prayer changes things." After attempting a more regular prayer life, I think we can also say, "Prayer changes *us!*" The men at The Master's Seminary, where my husband ministered, found this to be true as well. Every student is required to take a class on prayer, and the professor asks the men to pray for one hour a day for the duration of the semester. Is it any surprise to learn from the students' evaluations of their three years spent at seminary that, almost to a man, the prayer class truly changed their lives?

Blessing #2: Greater Purity

Yes, prayer changes lives, and one major change is greater purity. Becoming pure is a process of spiritual growth, and taking seriously the confession of sin during prayer time moves that process along, causing us to purge our life of practices that displease God. That's what happened to me when I began working on my prayer life.

For me, gossip was a serious struggle. Even though I knew God spoke specifically to women about not gossiping (1 Timothy 3:11 and Titus 2:3), I did it anyway. Convicted of my failure to follow God's guidelines and aware that my gossip didn't please God, I tried some practical remedies like taping little notes on the telephone (Is it true? Is it kind? Is it helpful?) and setting some self-imposed rules for my speech. I even prayed each day that I wouldn't gossip. And still I gossiped!

Real change began when I started not only to pray about gossip, but to confess it as an offense to God each time I did it. One day, about a month after I got serious about confession, I reached the height of my frustration. I was so sick of failing, sick of offending my Lord, and sick of confessing the sin of gossip every single day that I submitted myself to God for more radical surgery (Matthew 5:29-30). I asked Him to cut gossip out of my life. The Holy Spirit led me to that decision, guided that surgery, and has empowered the purification process. Let me quickly tell you that I've had my lapses, but still that day was a significant turning point for me. Purification—purging my life of a major sin (1 John 3:3)—took place, in part because I faced my sin regularly in prayer. Do you see the progression? Sin led to confession, which led to purging.

A Prayer for Purity

May I be incapable of rest or satisfaction of mind under a sense of Thy displeasure! Help me to clear accounts with thee....[4]

—Susanna Wesley

Blessing #3: Confidence in Making Decisions

How do you make decisions? I know how I used to make decisions before I learned to pray about them. Maybe you can relate. The phone would ring around nine in the morning. A woman would ask me to speak at her church, and, because I'd just eaten a scrambled egg and some toast, taken my thyroid pill, had a cup of coffee, and gone for a walk, I would be full of energy and blurt out, "Sure! When do you want me to come?" At four in the afternoon, the phone would ring again, another woman was calling with the same basic request, but, because it was the end

Make no decision without prayer.

of a long day and I was beat and ready to relax, I would answer this lady, "No way!" (My actual words were more gracious, but those were the words I was thinking.)

Why did I respond so differently? What criteria did I use for these decisions? In a word, *feelings*. While I was feeling full of fresh energy in the morning, my answer would be yes. In the late afternoon, when I was worn out, my answer would be no. My decisions were based on how I felt at the moment. I wasn't making spiritual decisions—I was making physical decisions.

This approach to decision-making changed as I began to write down in my special little book every decision I needed to make. I developed a motto for myself: *Make no decision without prayer*. Whatever option arose, I asked for time to pray about it first. The more important the decision, the more time I asked for. If there wasn't time for me to pray about it, I generally answered no because I wanted to be certain my decisions were actually God's choices for me. And I followed this approach for everything— invitations to showers, weddings, lunches, opportunities to minister, problems, ideas, crises, needs, dreams. I wrote down every decision I needed to make and took each one to God in prayer.

Imagine the difference this practice can make in a woman's life! The principle *make no decision without prayer* keeps me from rushing in and committing myself before I consult God. It guards me against people-pleasing (Galatians 1:10), and it ended my practice of making commitments and later calling to back out. Another benefit of praying first about my decisions is that my tendency to second-guess my commitments has stopped. As the events on my calendar approach, I feel no dread or fear or resentment. I don't wonder, "How did I get myself into this? What was I thinking when I said I'd do this? I wish I hadn't said yes." Instead I experience a solid confidence—confidence in *God*—and the excitement of anticipating what He will do at these events. A woman after God's own heart is a woman who will do *His* will (Acts 13:22)—not her own. The maxim *make no decision without prayer* has helped me do just that!

A Prayer for Direction

Forbid that I should venture on any business without first begging Thy direction and assistance.[5]

—Susanna Wesley

Blessing #4: Improved Relationships

Understandably prayer—specifically prayer for the people closest to us—strengthens our bonds with those dear people, but being a seeker of God's heart results in better relationships with people in general. How does this happen? These prayer principles, which I discovered as I began to pray regularly, help answer that question.

- *You cannot think about yourself and others at the same time*— As you and I settle our personal needs with God in private prayer, we can then rise up and focus all our attention outward—away from self and on to others.

- *You cannot hate the person you are praying for*—Jesus instructed us to pray for our enemies (Matthew 5:44), and God changes our hearts as we do so.

- *You cannot neglect the person you are praying for*—As we invest ourselves in prayer for other people, we find ourselves wonderfully involved in their lives.

An end to self-centeredness, the dissolution of ill will, and an end to neglect—these results of praying for someone will inevitably improve our relationship with him or her.

Blessing #5: Contentment

As the wife of a seminary student for ten years, I faced real challenges in the area of contentment, and a large source of frustration was our finances. While I lived in a tiny house with peeling paint and a living room ceiling about to cave in—and all Jim's income was designated for tuition, rent, and groceries—God dealt with me. I desperately needed His victory in the area of my heart's desires and dreams for our home and lives, and those needs pressed me to Him in prayer. Over and over again, day after day, I placed everything in God's hands, letting it be His job to meet those needs—and another prayer principle was born: *If He doesn't meet it, you didn't need it!* Through the years God has faithfully met the many needs of our family. We've experienced the reality of God's promise that no good thing will be withheld from those who walk uprightly (Psalm 84:11)—and you can too.

Blessing #6: God-Confidence

Dr. James Dobson wrote, "Believe it or not, low self-esteem was indicated as the most troubling problem by the majority of the women completing [his] questionnaire. More than 50 percent... marked this item above every other alternative on the list, and 80 percent placed it in the top five."[6] These women (and maybe you're one of them) could benefit from the tremendous *God*-confidence I began to enjoy as I kept cultivating a heart of prayer. And it's even better than self-confidence and self-esteem.

God-confidence comes as the Holy Spirit works in us. As we pray and when we make choices that honor God, the Holy Spirit fills us with His power for ministry. When we are filled with God's goodness, we are confidently and effectively able to share His love and joy. As women of prayer open to the transforming touch of the Holy Spirit, we will find His divine life in us overflowing into the lives of others.

> *There isn't time or space to list the many blessings that can be ours as we pray!*

Also, as a result of practicing the principle *make no decision without prayer,* we experience a divine assurance with every step we take. As the events we've prayed about and committed to arrive, we can enjoy the settled assurance that they are God's will, and we can therefore enter into them with delight, anticipation, and courage. We can truly serve the Lord with gladness (Psalm 100:2), not glumness. We can delight to do God's will (Psalm 40:8) instead of dreading it.

Blessing #7: The Ministry of Prayer

When I read Edith Schaeffer's book *Common Sense Christian Living,* I came across a concept that changed my life. While talking about prayer, Mrs. Schaeffer focused on the mind-boggling fact that prayer makes a difference in history. She wrote, "Interceding for other people makes a difference in the history of other people's lives."[7] Looking at the life of the apostle Paul, she noted that he always asked others to pray for him because he expected "a difference to take place…in answer to prayer. Paul expect[ed] history to be different because intercession [was] taken seriously as an important task."[8]

This mature understanding of prayer encouraged me in two distinct ways. First, I came to grips with the power of prayer to change lives. I knew from experience that prayer had changed my life, but...the lives of others? That idea was new to me. It seemed impossible, but Mrs. Schaeffer assured me that even I, a young Christian, could have a role in the mysterious ways of God. She helped me believe that my infant prayers could make a difference in history!

The second revelation was recognizing prayer as a ministry, which was an important realization for me. At the time I was a mother with two little ones at home, and I felt left out at church. I struggled because I couldn't attend all the wonderful women's studies and events, even though I knew my place at that time was at home. Coming face-to-face with the fact that prayer is a ministry ended my feelings of uselessness and ineffectiveness. The blank-paged book Katherine gave to me was key to the beginning of my prayer ministry. I used that book to jot down the names of our staff at church, the missionaries we knew, and the requests shared by others. My heart took flight as I joined God in the vital ministry of prayer!

There isn't time or space to list the many blessings that can be yours and mine as we pray. I've only shared a very few! But I know that as you bow your knees and heart before God and begin cultivating a heart of prayer, you will taste and know that the Lord is good (Psalm 34:8).

Yes, But How?

How can we cultivate a heart of prayer and enjoy the blessings that accompany a life of committed and devoted prayer? Here are some quick thoughts.

- Start a prayer log to record requests and responses as you travel your own personal journey of prayer.

- Set aside some time each day to linger with the Lord in

prayer and remember that *something is better than nothing.* Begin small—and watch for the mighty effects!

- Pray always (Ephesians 6:18) and in all places, enjoying God's presence with you wherever you go (Joshua 1:9).

- Pray faithfully for others—including your enemies (Matthew 5:44).

- Take seriously the powerful privilege of the ministry of prayer.

Heart Response

First things first! Of course you and I want our relationship with God to have the reigning position in our hearts. I know that, like me, you want to walk so closely with Him that His fragrance permeates all of your life and refreshes all who cross your path. This happens when you meet with God in prayer, prostrate in soul and humble in heart.

So, dear praying friend, no matter where we are—at home or in another country, in the car or in the shower, in a wheelchair or in the hospital, sitting alone or in a room with thousands of people—you and I can be in tune with God through prayer. We can also lift countless others toward heaven and boldly ask our omnipotent God to make a difference in their lives. I pray you will take this powerful privilege—and responsibility!—seriously.

Now think about this: Do you think praying—even for just five minutes a day—could change your life? It can! Lingering in God's presence through prayer will increase your faith in Him, provide a place for you to unload your burdens, remind you that God is always near, and help you not to panic. It is one way God has provided for us to commune with Him. And when you accept His invitation to commune with Him, He will transform your heart and change your life.

4

A Heart That Obeys

I have found David…
a man after My own heart,
who will do all My will.
ACTS 13:22

Watching my daughters grow into responsible women has been a constant delight to me as a mother. Now that they've become adults and ventured out on their own, I hope and pray that I've given them enough of the basics to build their lives on—the basics of faith in Christ, the basics of homemaking, and the basics of cooking. One night, though, I wasn't so sure.

For several years Katherine enjoyed the fun and fellowship of sharing an apartment with some young women from our church. Part of the adventure was cooking for the group on her assigned nights. But when she began to date her Paul (who is now her husband), the two of them spent many an evening at our home "hanging out" with Jim and me. On one of those nights Katherine decided to dig out a smudged old recipe—a long-time family favorite—and bake some brownies to top off our evening. Because

I don't normally make them for just Jim and me, we could hardly wait for those brownies to cool down enough to eat them with tall glasses of cold milk!

> The heart God delights in is compliant, cooperative, and responsive to Him and His commands.

Finally we each had a huge, warm brownie to bite into—but after one taste we knew we wouldn't be taking a second bite. Something was missing. Not wanting to hurt Katherine's feelings, we took turns mumbling something somewhat kind like, "Hmmm, these taste different..." or "Hmmm, they sure do *smell* good..." and "Oh, Kath, thanks for making us brownies." Finally I asked her if she might have left anything out. With all of the gusto in the world, she cheerfully volunteered, "Oh yes, I left out the salt! At the apartment I've been learning to cook without salt. Salt's bad for us." Those brownies had to be thrown out because a single missing ingredient—a little teaspoon of salt—kept them from being edible.

Just as a batch of brownies requires several ingredients to become what we intend it to be, several ingredients are key to us becoming women after God's own heart. We've already talked about devotion to God, devotion to His Word, and devotion to prayer. But one more ingredient—as important as salt in brownies—goes into making you and me women after God's own heart, and that is obedience. The heart God delights in is a heart that is compliant, cooperative, and responsive to Him and His commands—a heart that obeys.

Two Kinds of Hearts

The title for this book—*A Woman After God's Own Heart*—is drawn from God's description of King David. God testified,

"I have found David…a man after My own heart, who will do all My will" (Acts 13:22). These words were spoken in startling contrast to the character of the reigning king of Israel, Saul.

Here's a little background information. Speaking on behalf of God, the prophet Samuel rebuked Saul for failing to obey God's specific instructions (1 Samuel 13). Again and again, as reported in 1 Samuel, Saul overstepped his bounds, the ones God set for him. On several occasions he specifically disobeyed God. Although he was very careful to offer prescribed sacrifices to God, Saul failed to offer God the ultimate sacrifice—obedience from a heart wholly devoted to Him (1 Samuel 15:22). Clearly Saul was not responsive to God or His laws.

Finally, after one extremely serious act of disobedience, God sent Samuel to Saul with a twofold message: "Your kingdom shall not continue" and "The LORD has sought for Himself a man after His own heart" (1 Samuel 13:14). God was communicating something along this order—"Saul, you're through as king. I've put up with your rebellious, unresponsive heart long enough, and now I've found just the right man to serve me. This man who will take your place is a man with a responsive heart, a man with a heart of obedience, a man who will follow all my commands, fulfill all my desires, and do all my will."

Here we witness two very different kinds of hearts—the heart of David and the heart of Saul.

- In his heart, David was willing to obey, but Saul was satisfied with merely external acts of sacrifice.

- David served God. Saul served himself and did things his way.

- David was concerned with following God's will, but Saul cared solely for his own will.

- David's heart was centered on God, and Saul's was centered on Saul.

- Even though David didn't always obey God, he had what mattered over the long haul—a heart after God. In sharp contrast, Saul's devotion to God was impulsive and sporadic.

- Although David was well-known for his physical prowess and might as a warrior, he was humbly dependent upon God, trusting in Him and repeatedly acknowledging, "The Lord is the strength of my life" (Psalm 27:1). Saul, on the other hand, was proud. He relied on his own skill, his own wisdom and judgment, and his arm of flesh.

God gave both of these kings opportunities to lead Israel, but in the end they walked down different paths—Saul away from God and David toward Him. Saul's heart was unresponsive to God's will, while David's was devoted to obedience. They were like two different musicians, one who sits down at a piano and plunks on it, here a little, there a little (almost everyone can play "chopsticks") and the other who sits for hours at a time, a disciplined, faithful, and dedicated student. The first creates immature, irregular, discordant sounds that fade away, while the other learns, grows, excels, and lifts the hearts and souls of others as he fine tunes himself to the Almighty. Saul's song—his walk with the Lord—was impulsive, transitory, and undeveloped. But David, the sweet psalmist of Israel, offered up to God the purest melodies of devoted love and committed obedience. Truly, his was a heart after God!

Yes, But How?

How can we follow after David in our devotion to God? What

can we do so that God can grow in us hearts committed to obedience? A heart committed to doing God's will is an important ingredient when it comes to living out our love for God.

God calls us to take care of our hearts. As I noted earlier, God tells us to "keep your heart with all diligence, for out of it spring the issues of life" (Proverbs 4:23). As we walk this path of life, God says we are to ponder the path of our feet (verse 26) and look straight ahead, not side to side (verse 25). Rather than turning to the right or to the left (verse 27), we are to follow ways that are established by God (verse 26). The key, God says, to living a life of obedience—a life that stays on His path—is the heart. If we keep our hearts, if we diligently attend to them and guard them, then all of the issues, the actions, the "ongoings and the out-goings" of life will be handled God's way.[1] A heart responsive to God and His ways leads to a life of obedience—and these proven guidelines can help us stay on God's path.

Concentrate on doing what is right—When God looked into David's heart, He saw what He wants to see in us—a heart that will do His will. A wholehearted love for God looks to Him through His Word and prayer, always watching and waiting, ever ready to do what He says, prepared to act on His expressed desires. Such a heart—tender and teachable—will concentrate on doing what is right.

> *Let God lead you on His path so you can be sure you're doing the right thing.*

But what about those situations where you're not sure what is right? In your heart you want to do the right thing, but you're just not sure what that right thing is. First, don't do anything until you know what is right. Ask God for guidance. Take time to pray, to think, to search the Scriptures, and to ask advice from someone more seasoned in Christ. If a person is asking you to do something you are unsure of, simply say, "I'm going to have to give this some thought and prayer. I'll let you know later." Do nothing until you know what the right thing is.

Besides, consider the following Scriptures. We are told, "In all your ways acknowledge Him, and He shall direct your paths" (Proverbs 3:6). We also know that "if any of you lacks wisdom, let him ask of God…and it will be given to him" (James 1:5). Also, act on the truth of James 4:17—"To him who knows to do good [to do the right thing] and does not do it, to him it is sin." Look to God and pray, "I don't want to sin so I have to know what the right thing, the good thing, is. Please, what is the right thing?" Let God lead you on His path so you can be sure you are doing the right thing. The bottom line? When in doubt, don't (Romans 14:23). Or, put another way, when in doubt, it's out!

Cease doing what is wrong—The split second you think or do anything contrary to God's heart, stop immediately! (Such action is key to training your heart to be responsive to God.) Just put the skids on the activity. If it's gossip, stop. If it's an unworthy thought, stop (Philippians 4:8). If there's a spark of anger in your heart, stop before you act on it. If you've spoken an unedifying word, stop before you speak another. If you've said yes to something but you're not at peace about that decision, stop. Or if you get into a situation that turns out to be sinful or something you didn't plan on, stop and get out!

Everyone has experiences like these. They happen every day. And how you respond reveals what's at the core of your heart. Ceasing an activity or thought process before sin progresses any further turns your heart right back around toward God and puts you back on His path. So call on the Lord. He will give you strength…whatever the temptation, whatever the dangerous path (Hebrews 2:18).

Confess any wrong—Because Christ covered our sins by His blood through His death, you and I are forgiven. We may not *feel* forgiven—but you and I only need to *know* that we are. But we still keep sinning. So when I've done something contrary to God's Word, I've learned to acknowledge in my heart, "This is wrong. This is sin! I can't do this!" After all, "if we say that we have no sin, we deceive ourselves, and the truth is not in us" (1 John 1:8). So I call sin "sin," and by doing so I train my heart to be more responsive to God's convicting Spirit.

When you and I confess our sins like that, God "is faithful and just to forgive us our sins and to cleanse us from all unrighteousness" (1 John 1:9)—and the sooner we confess, the better! And as you confess your sin, be sure you're also forsaking it. Proverbs 28:13 warns, "He who covers his sins will not prosper, but whoever confesses *and* forsakes them will have mercy." Don't be like the farmer who said, "I want to confess that I stole some hay from my neighbor." When the clergyman asked, "How much did you steal?" the farmer declared, "I stole half a load, but make it a whole load. I'm going back to get the other half tonight!"

Clear up things with others—Confession makes things right with God, but if we've hurt another person, we need to clear things up with that person too. When it is appropriate, we need to admit our wrongful behavior to the person involved…something I had to do the first morning I sang in our church choir. A sweet woman reached out to me, smiled, and asked, "Hi! Are you one of the new guys?" For whatever reason, I snapped, "No, but I'm one of the new *girls*." As I spoke those words, I was immediately convicted, but we were filing in to sing, to worship! I limped through all those moving (and convicting!) hymns about our precious Jesus. Finally I got back into the choir room and apologized. I waited until the woman I had been so mean to got there and then said, "I really have a smart mouth, don't I? I'm sorry I responded to your kindness with such a smart remark. Will you please forgive me?"

Continue on as soon as possible—Our enemy Satan delights when our failure to obey God keeps us from serving Him. You and I can all too easily wallow in the fact that we've failed God and then allow our emotions to keep us from going on and following after Him. Oh, we know we are forgiven. And we've stopped the behavior, acknowledged and confessed our sin, forsaken our thoughts or actions, and cleared up the situation. But we still say to ourselves, "I can't believe I did that, said that, thought that, acted like that. How could I have done that? I'm unworthy. I am totally unfit to serve God."

When that's the case, we need to turn to another truth from God's Word and let it lift us up, dust us off, refresh us, and set us back on His path. Speaking divine directions to us through His Spirit, God encourages us—those of us who have confessed our disobedience and been forgiven—to be "forgetting those things which are behind and reaching forward to those things which are ahead...[and pressing] toward the goal for the prize of the upward call of God in Christ Jesus" (Philippians 3:13-14). Once we've acknowledged and dealt with our failure to follow God wholeheartedly, once we've addressed our acts of disobedience, you and I are to forget those things from the past and go on. Oh, we are to remember the lessons learned, but we are also to train our hearts to obey by obeying this command from God to go on.

Heart Response

Now, dear follower of God, we've come to the end of the first section of this book. And what we've learned about our hearts will help us determine to follow the path God lays out for us in the chapters to follow. We're preparing to examine other aspects of our busy and complicated daily life in the pages ahead, but before we step away from focusing on our relationship with God, you (and I) need to take a serious look at our own hearts.

Obedience is a foundational stepping-stone on the path of God's will—the path you'll be following as a woman after His heart. Sure footing here will prepare you to respond later to what God has to say. So right now consider whether your heart is totally in God's hands. Have you yielded your will to Him? When God looks into your heart, does He easily see your willingness to obey Him?

In Saul's day, God declared that He is looking for a heart that will obey Him, that will do all His will. Do those words describe your heart? Is God's desire your desire? Does your heart follow hard after God (Psalm 63:8), close to Him, on His heels, literally clinging to Him?[2]

Can you pinpoint any behavior in your life that calls for a heart response of confession and a change of location onto the path of obedience? If so, stop right now, acknowledge that area of disobedience, confess that sin, choose to forsake that behavior, and then step right back onto God's path of beauty, peace, and joy. As you desire all that God desires, love all that He loves, and humble yourself under His mighty hand (1 Peter 5:6), then your heart will indeed be a heart after God. What a blessed thought!

Part 2

The Pursuit
of God's Priorities

5

A Heart That Serves

I will make him a helper.
GENESIS 2:18

It was a bright autumn day at the University of Oklahoma. As I hurried toward my first class after lunch, I noticed him again. He was smiling as he came my way. Every Monday, Wednesday, and Friday our paths crossed as he too rushed to class. His name— Jim George—was unknown to me at the time, but he looked extremely nice, he was cute, and I loved his smile! Well, evidently he noticed me too because soon a mutual friend set up a blind date for us.

That was in November 1964. On Valentine's Day we were engaged, and our wedding took place the first weekend school was out, June 1, 1965. That was more than 40 years ago—and I wish I could say, "That was 40-plus wonderful, blissful, happy years ago," but I can't. You see, Jim and I began our marriage without God, and that meant rough times. From the beginning we fumbled, we argued, and we let each other down. Because we didn't find fulfillment in our marriage, we poured our lives into causes, friends, hobbies, and intellectual pursuits. Having two children also didn't fill the emptiness we each felt. Our married life droned on for eight frustrating years until, by an act of God's grace, we became a Christian family, a family centered on Jesus Christ as the head, a family with the Bible to guide us.

Giving our lives to Jesus Christ made a tremendous difference inside our hearts, but how would Christ change our marriage? We each had been given new life in Christ, but what were we going to do about the tension in our marriage and therefore in our home?

I had much to learn about being a woman, a wife, a mother who pleased God, and thankfully—soon after naming Jesus as my Lord and Savior—I had in my hands a calendar for reading through the Bible. On January 1, 1974, I began to follow that schedule, and as I read I did something that I recommend you do too. I marked every passage that spoke to me as a woman with a pink highlighter.

Well, God went to work on my makeover that very day. On January 1, my first day of reading, I came across the first aspect of my job assignment as a Christian wife—I was to serve Jim, to help him. I marked these words in Genesis 2:18 in pink:

> It is not good that man should be alone;
> I will make him a helper comparable to him.

Called to Serve

To begin our discussion we must realize that a woman after God's own heart is a woman who carefully cultivates a servant spirit, whether she is married or not. She desires to follow in the steps of Jesus, who "did not come to be served, but to serve" (Matthew 20:28). Such following calls for lifelong attention to the heart attitude of serving.

And if you are a married woman, that attitude and service starts at home with your family. And more specifically, with your husband. God has designed the wife to be her husband's helper. So the first step on my journey of a thousand miles to becoming God's kind of wife was beginning to understand that *I am on assignment from God to help my husband.*

Exactly what is this "helper" from Genesis 2:18, I wondered. Borrowing a few of Jim's Bible-study books, I learned that a helper is one who shares man's responsibilities, responds to his nature with understanding and love, and wholeheartedly cooperates with him in working out the plan of God.[1] Anne Ortlund talks about becoming a team with your husband, pointing out that being a team eliminates any sense of competition between spouses. Writing about this partnership of marriage, she describes a wife being solidly behind and supportive of her husband. She declares, "I have no desire to run parallel to Ray, sprinting down the track in competition. I want to be behind him, encouraging him."[2]

> *A servant spirit helps me be more like Christ as I esteem others— especially my husband— as better than myself and commit myself to service.*

I can honestly say that I became a better wife—and a better Christian—when I became a better helper. Realizing *I am on assignment from God to help my husband* opened my eyes. According to God's plan, I was not to compete with Jim or impede his progress. Instead, I am to be solidly behind him and supportive of him—helping him.

Because my husband was a leader in our church, I read many

books about leaders' wives, hoping to learn from them more about how to support and encourage Jim. Reading about the wife of former President Dwight D. Eisenhower, gave me further insight into the attitude of a helper. Julie Nixon Eisenhower explained, "Mamie had seen her role as one of emotional support for her husband....She had no interest in promoting herself. Most of all, she was the woman behind the man, the woman who proudly proclaimed, 'Ike was my career.' "[3]

As God impressed on my heart the importance of a servant spirit, especially in my role as a helper to my husband, I wrote out a prayer of commitment. As I did, I stepped back a few paces to ensure that, in my own heart, Jim was clearly in front and I was definitely stationed behind him to help. On that day—and in that prayer to God—I began a life of serving Jim that has continued for more than three decades. Oh, I have many things to do! What woman and wife doesn't? But my primary purpose and role each day is to help Jim, to share his responsibilities, to respond to his nature, and to wholeheartedly cooperate with him in God's plan for our life together.

This mind-set, this servant spirit, helps me be more like Christ as I esteem others—especially my husband—as better than myself (Philippians 2:3) and commit myself to service.

Yes, But How?

How can we develop a heart committed to service, a heart intent on emulating Christ in service to another person? What can a wife do so that God can grow in her a heart committed to helping her husband? Consider these suggestions.

Make a commitment to help your husband—I had to ask myself, Would I or wouldn't I try to become a helper? Would I or wouldn't

I follow God's plan for me to help my husband? The decision was mine. And it's yours too. And when you do decide to do it God's way, you might want to write your own prayer of commitment to God like I did. It was a lifesaver—and a cheerleader—when my energy and understanding fell short. Let your words reflect your decision to help your husband, to be a team with him, and to make helping him the priority focus of your every day.

Focus on your husband—God wants us wives to focus our energy and efforts on our husbands. Each of us is to focus on *his* tasks, *his* goals, *his* responsibilities. I know firsthand this can be an area of struggle because our sin nature cries out, "Me first!" But God wants us to say, "You first!" when it comes to our husbands. So periodically ask yourself about your marriage, "Who's Number One?"

One practical way I try to help Jim by focusing on him and his responsibilities is by asking him two questions every day:

"What can I do for you today?"

"What can I do to help you make better use of your time today?"

You may worry (as I did initially) about what major, time-consuming demands your husband might make. But I have to tell you the first time I asked Jim these questions all he wanted was a button sewn on his favorite sports coat. That's all! And it was no problem for me to whip out a needle and thread and make Jim my Number One human priority by sewing on a little button.

Sometimes, though, the requests are larger. For instance, I remember a week of "larger" demands as Jim prepared to go to Germany for five months with his Army Reserve unit. His days were full of physicals...while I ran to the safe deposit box for wills, birth certificates, and our marriage license. He had dental visits and blood typing...while I looked up mortgage records, worked on his passport, and set up an email account. He was also fixing up the house and organizing his job before he left the country—and all this as one of my book deadlines rapidly approached.

But even when I don't like how the day unfolds or the answers Jim gives to my two questions (I now know his answers can change the pattern of my entire day!), I do want Jim to be my highest human priority. And I want him to know he is. After all, that's my assignment from God—to ease my husband's life by helping him.

And even if there is no husband in your life today, you can nurture a heart of Christlike service as you focus on helping and serving other people. Whether you are married or not, serving the people in your life is part of God's will for you. It pleases Him when you follow His will, benefits the lives of those you serve, and shows Christ to the world.

Ask of your actions, Will this help or hinder my husband?— That simple question can be a good lens through which to look at how we act in our marriages. Let me give you a simple example. Your husband's boss asks him to go on a business trip, and you pout and punish him because he has to go. Does that help your husband or hinder him?

When my husband became a full-time seminary student *and* a full-time staff member at church *and* traveled extensively with our missions pastor, I read every book I could find about Mrs. Ruth Graham, wife of evangelist Billy Graham. Because her famous husband was absent from home almost ten months a year, I learned much from her about being alone. Listen to this wise statement from her: "We have to learn to make the least of all that goes and the most of all that comes."[4] This encouragement from a fellow helper made me a better helper to Jim as he prepared for each trip (even a five-month trip to Germany!) and decreased my urge to pout and punish.

Here's another example. Your husband has told you the state of the budget, but you want something right away and are pushing to get it. I know that situation well from experience. We had lived in our home (the one with the peeling paint and the sagging ceiling!) for more than a decade, and it was finally time to do some remodeling. I was ecstatic. To me, a fireplace had been the one thing missing in our charming little house all these years, and this was our opportunity to install one. But Jim sat down and clearly showed me there wasn't enough money in our loan to add a fireplace.

But oh how I wanted that fireplace. So I said things like, "Wouldn't this be a great evening for a fire in a fireplace...if we had one?" and "Just think...if we had a fireplace, we could put some logs on and have dinner in front of a warm fire!"

Is your heart committed to service—specifically to serve and help your husband?

But then I asked the question, "Elizabeth, are you helping or hindering?" And I knew the answer immediately (and so do you)! One day God helped me realize I was nagging, and I committed before the Lord not to mention a fireplace to Jim again...ever. I wrote out that commitment in yet another prayer to God, and—thanks to God's grace—I *never* talked about a fireplace again.

And another example. Your husband thinks your family should move so he can better provide for the family, and you either don't want to move or you firmly declare, "Not there!" As a pastor, my husband counseled a couple in this situation. The husband was a truck driver who wanted to change careers because of the wear and tear it put on their marriage (the reason they had come for counseling in the first place). A terrific job opportunity finally opened up for him half a state away where they could afford to purchase a home and begin their family. Sharon, however, didn't want to move. She loved her job and was next in line for a significant promotion at work. But realizing God's plan that she help her husband—who was trying his best to provide *financially* through a better job and *spiritually* through a better situation for their marriage—enabled her to help, and not hinder, his leadership. They made the move—and oh, what an abundance of blessings God had waiting for this precious couple in their new hometown.

And one more example. Your husband wants to have a daily time reading the Bible together as a family, but you don't want to...or you don't want to study what he has chosen...or you never quite get up early enough to have breakfast ready in time to allow for family devotions. In most families the wife is usually responsible for the morning schedule at home. And because she controls the schedule, she has the ability to make a family worship time happen—or not happen. If her heart is committed to service, she has the power to help her husband accomplish this goal and others.

Is yours a heart committed to service, specifically to serving and helping your husband? What an abundance of blessings God has waiting for *you* when yours is such a heart!

Heart Response

Helping. It's a simple and noble assignment—and it reaps rich rewards. Living out God's assignment certainly benefits our husbands and anyone else we serve, but we benefit as well as we learn to serve as Christ did. Being a servant is a sign of Christian maturity. It is the true mark of Christ (Philippians 2:7), who served to the point of death (Matthew 20:28). So how do you measure up as a helper? In your marriage, do you see yourself as a team player, free of any competitive actions, thoughts, or desires? Is bettering your husband's life your primary concern? Is helping your husband the main focus of your energy? Have you committed your heart to following God's plan for you, His plan that you help and not hinder your husband? As you and I promote the well being of our husbands—and of the multitude of other people God has placed in our lives—our service glorifies God.

6

A Heart That Follows

Wives, submit to your own husbands.
EPHESIANS 5:22

Having started down the road toward becoming my husband's helper, I kept reading my Bible. As I did so, I discovered more to my role of wife, and I saw other qualities I needed if I were to be the kind of wife God wants me to be. In fact, the number of times my pink marker hit the pages showed me I had a lot of work to do. The next big item I noticed was *I am on assignment from God to follow my husband's leadership.*

As a new Christian, I found what the Bible refers to as "submission" to my husband and following his leadership to be a foreign concept. Therefore I had to do some research. When I did, I learned that in the Bible "submission" (*hupotasso*) is primarily a military term meaning to rank oneself under someone else. This heart attitude is lived out by leaving things to the judgment of another person and yielding or deferring to the opinion or authority of someone else.[1]

As I said, the concept was new and I felt my heart hesitating. But I kept studying (and praying to be a woman—and wife—after God's own heart), and the Bible helped flesh out the heart attitude that God desires in His women. Here's what I found.

"Be Submissive One to Another"

First, I discovered the fact that the Christian lifestyle—for men as well as women—is one of submission. You and I are called to be "submitting to one another" (Ephesians 5:21). God's desire for us—married or single, young or old, male or female—is to honor, serve, and subject ourselves to one another. We as Christians are to…

- "submit…to everyone who works and labors with us" (1 Corinthians 16:16).
- be "submitting to one another in the fear of God" (Ephesians 5:21).
- "obey those who rule over you, and be submissive" (Hebrews 13:17).
- "submit to God" (James 4:7).
- "submit yourselves to every ordinance of man for the Lord's sake, whether to the king as supreme, or to governors…for this is the will of God" (1 Peter 2:13-15).
- "be submissive to your masters [employers]" (1 Peter 2:18).
- "all of you be submissive to one another" (1 Peter 5:5).

It's clear that we reflect Christ's character as we move away from selfishness and, acting out of honor for other people, defer to them. A heart willing to follow and submit, dedicated to honoring and yielding to others, is to be the heart of God's people, His church, and His women.

And that includes wives to husbands—"Wives, submit to your own husbands" (Ephesians 5:22 and Colossians 3:18). When it comes to marriage, God arranged for the sake of order that the husband lead and the wife follow. For marriages to run smoothly, God has said, "The head of every man is Christ, the head of woman is man, and the head of Christ is God" (1 Corinthians 11:3).

Now don't be alarmed. The husband's headship doesn't mean we wives can't offer wise input (Proverbs 31:26), enter into a discussion, or ask questions for clarification during the decision-making process. But the

God, the perfect Artist, designed marriage to be beautiful, natural, and functional by giving it a single head, the husband.

husband's headship does mean that he is responsible for the final decision. Author Elisabeth Elliot describes her father's headship in her childhood home. She writes, " 'Head of the house' did not mean that our father barked out orders, threw his weight around, and demanded submission from his wife. It simply meant that he was the one finally responsible."[2]

In the end, the husband is accountable to God for his leadership decisions, and we are accountable to God for how we follow that leadership. Our husbands answer to God for leading, and we answer to Him for following. Now I ask you, which responsibility would you rather have?

God's instruction that the man lead and the woman follow results in *beauty* as well as order. I remember as a child seeing the stuffed "head" of a goat in a museum—only it had two heads. It was abnormal, grotesque, a freak attraction, an oddity—and so is a marriage with two heads. But God, the perfect Artist, designed marriage to be beautiful, natural, and functional by giving it a single head, the husband. Thank You, Lord, that marriage is Your work of art.

The Privilege of Choice

Another translation—and yet another pink passage—showed me that I am responsible for whether or not I submit. It said, "Wives, submit [or subject] *yourselves* unto your own husbands, as unto the Lord" (Ephesians 5:22 kjv).

That means submission is a wife's choice. She decides whether or not to follow her husband. No one can do it for her, and no one can make her do it. Her husband can't make her submit and follow, her church can't make her, her pastor can't make her, and neither can a counselor. She must decide to choose to defer to her husband and follow his leadership.

I gasped—and grew as a Christian wife—when I read about four women just like you and me who were meeting each week to study the Bible. One week they happened upon 1 Corinthians 11:3, a verse about the headship of the husband in marriage. This is the verse we just considered that tells us, "The head of every man is Christ, the head of woman is man, and the head of Christ is God." Coming face to face with God's plan called them to make some decisions, some choices.

> The leader for that evening read [the verse] aloud, paused, and read it again…Every one of those women—they all knew it—was the head in her marriage…
> Someone said weakly, "Does St. Paul say anything else about [headship and submission]?" An index

was consulted, and the other Pauline statements (Colossians 3:18; Ephesians 5:22ff.; 1 Timothy 2:11ff.) were read out. There was some discussion. Finally the leader said, "Well, girls—what do we do?" Someone else said, "We've *got* to do it."…

Then came the miracle. In less than a year the four women, with amazement and delight, were telling each other and every other woman they knew what had happened. The husbands, all four, had quietly taken over…and, with no exceptions, every one of the women felt her marriage had come to a new depth of happiness—a joy—that it had never had before. A *rightness.*

Seeing this astonishing thing that not one of them had thought possible…the four wives one day realized an astonishing further truth: they realized that their husbands had never demanded and would never have demanded the headship; it could only be a free gift from wife to husband.[3]

Are you giving the gift of headship? Are you experiencing the rightness that comes from a decision to follow God's plan for marriage? Are you using your privilege of choice to follow God… and your husband?

An Important Distinction

The "who" of submission for a wife is clear in Ephesians 5:22— "Wives, submit to your *own husbands*," not to other people we admire and respect. And this is an important distinction.

A Christian woman, married to a man who was not a believer, came to me for some counsel. Sue wanted to quit her job and attend Bible college for four years in preparation for entering full-time Christian work. After telling me her heart's longings, I asked her, "Well, Sue, what does your husband say about this?" She quickly answered, "Oh, he doesn't want me to do it."

"Why, Sue," I exclaimed, "God has spoken!" You see, God's plan for marriage is that each wife honor and follow her husband. When Sue talked about her dream with her pastor and her Christian employer, both of them told her to go ahead with her plans. She was all too ready to honor the guidance of others. But the Bible is clear. We are to submit to our own husbands.

Believe me, I know that sometimes we're tempted to dismiss God's plan. We say or think things like, "My husband isn't walking with God, so I don't have to submit to him" or "My husband isn't a Christian, so I don't have to submit to him." The apostle Peter wrote the following words to help women in those exact situations, women with unbelieving and/or disobedient husbands: "Wives, likewise, be submissive to your own husbands, that even if some do not obey the word, they, without a word [from their wives], may be won by the conduct of their wives" (1 Peter 3:1). In other words, our submission to our husbands preaches a lovelier and more powerful sermon than our mouths ever could. Conduct counts!

It's important to mention here the one exception to following your husband's advice, and that is if he asks you to violate some teaching from God's Word. If he's asking you to do something illegal or immoral, go to a trusted pastor or counselor and follow the advice you receive there.

Looking Up Helps

Ephesians 5:22 also gives us the "how" of submission—"Wives, submit [or subject] to your own husbands, *as to the Lord.*" As soon as I stopped thinking about following Jim and started looking up and thinking about following the Lord, my struggle to submit slowly began to abate. I sort of mentally set Jim to one side, and that left me staring straight into the Lord's face. Suddenly following Jim became much simpler—and easier. It had nothing to do with Jim and everything to do with the Lord. As a familiar Scripture says, "Whatever you do [and I added in my heart and mind the words "including following my husband!"], do it heartily, *as to the Lord* and not to men" (Colossians 3:23). So if you're struggling, look up, dear one. Remind yourself it's *Him* (the Lord), not him (your husband)!

Something to Think About

Here's something else to think about. What is the scope of our submission to our husbands? On what matters, decisions, and situations are we to submit? How would you answer these questions after reading this scripture? "Let the wives be [subject] to their own husbands in *everything*" (Ephesians 5:24). So whenever I'm tempted to say "Yes, but…" or "But what if…" I try to remember those two little words—"in everything." Those two words cover large and small issues alike. Case in point…

After the massive rumblings of the 1994 California earthquake, Jim and I went together to select lamps to replace those that had broken. We were delighted to find an affordable Tiffany glass table lamp. But when we got our lamp home, my heart sank as I opened the box and saw the faded, washed-out colors. They were nothing like those on the model. The pastel greens and pinks would never do in our forest-green library. But Jim thought it looked okay and said there was no reason to take it back. It was definitely not easy, but I said nothing, regarding this as another opportunity to submit to my own husband...as to the Lord...in everything...and without a word.

Granted, the lamp is a small thing, but such small things are a good place to start submitting "in everything." We'll get to some larger things later, but at this point ask God to give you His grace the next time a small thing comes your way.

But wait! That's not the end of my story. Here's what happened next. One day I smelled something burning, followed my nose, and found smoke rising out of that new lamp, caused by an electrical shortage in its wiring. Racing to unplug it from the wall, I noticed that the glass panels were completely blackened from the smoke and the current. The end of the story? We took the lamp back, got a full refund, and purchased another lamp...with the rich colors I had wanted in the first place. Jim was honored, I grew in grace, and God supplied another lamp. I hope and pray that, in time, you have many such wonderful stories about God's grace and His enablement of your choices to follow and honor your husband.

A Life of Faith

Do you know the main reason why we wives hesitate to follow our husband's leadership? God says it's *fear*. We are afraid of what will happen if our husbands do things their way instead of our way...or another way. Clearly, underneath God's call to us to submit lies a much deeper, more fundamental call to live a life of faith in God. "The holy women" of the Bible "who *trusted in God* also adorned themselves, being submissive to their own husbands," and we can follow in their steps if we "do good and are *not afraid with any terror*" (1 Peter 3:5-6).

Faith is the opposite of fear (Mark 4:40), but how does faith fit with following a husband's leadership? It is by faith that you and

I believe God works in our lives directly through our husbands. It is by faith in our sovereign God that we trust that God knows our husbands' decisions and the end results of those decisions, and trusting that God redeems, if not guides, those decisions. And so it is by faith in God that our fear is dispelled and we gain the strength to submit. Why not ask God, as the disciples did, to increase your faith (Luke 17:5)?

The Root...The Motive for Submission

Perhaps the Scripture that reached deepest into my heart as God's call to submission was taking root in my heart was this one—"Admonish the young women to...[be] obedient to their own husbands, *that the word of God may not be blasphemed*" (Titus 2:4-5), meaning discredited or dishonored. As I pondered this verse, the idea of following my husband's leadership suddenly leaped into the heavenly realm, rising far above all my earthly, petty, selfish, and fleshly excuses for not wanting to let Jim lead.

Once again it became clear to me that following Jim had nothing to do with him and everything to do with *Him*—with God! God has instituted it, commanded it, and given me the faith in Him to be able to obey His Word—and He is honored when I do. My respect and deference to my husband testifies to all who are watching that God's Word and His way are right. That makes God's call to nurture hearts that follow our husbands a high calling indeed.

Yes, But How?

How does a wife follow her husband? Here are some steps I have taken.

Dedicate your heart to honoring your husband—Change requires a decision, and that's definitely the case with submission. You and I have to decide to follow our husbands, make up our minds to practice (or work on!) it, and dedicate our hearts to honoring God and our husbands in this way.

Remember to respect—Develop the basic heart attitude of respect. Doing so helps us in the practice of following. God states, "Let the wife see that she *respects* her husband" (Ephesians 5:33). God isn't telling us to *feel* respect, but to *show* respect, to act with respect. A good way to measure our respect for our husbands is to answer the question, *Am I treating my husband as I would treat Christ?*

You reveal your respect for your husband in little daily acts. Do you, for instance, ask your husband to do something—or do you tell him? Do you stop, look, and listen to him when he's talking? Do you speak about him with respect to your children, your parents, and others?

Respond to your husband's words and actions positively—Ooooh, submission came hard for me! So when I first became a believer in Christ, I had much to learn from God and the lovely women I met at my church. Old ways die hard. I would buck, snort, kick, and fight (at least in my spirit!) with Jim about everything—which lane he should drive in, whether or not we got donuts on the way to church on Sunday morning, his method of disciplining the children versus mine, how he should handle his ministry. On and on our struggles went. I knew what Scripture said. In fact, I'd even memorized the passages we've been considering. But I still struggled. For me the breakthrough came with developing a positive response. I trained—yes, trained—myself to respond positively to anything and everything my husband said or did. And the training was a two-phase process.

Phase One: Say nothing!—Have you ever been in the presence of a woman who doesn't respect her husband? She nags at him, picks on him, and disagrees with him in public. She corrects him, battling with him over every little thing ("No, Harry, it wasn't eight years ago. It was seven years ago"). Or she cuts him off, interrupts, or, worse, finishes his sentences for him.

Clearly, saying nothing is a great improvement over that kind of behavior. Saying nothing is also a giant step toward learning submission. All we have to do to give a positive response is keep our mouths closed and say nothing. It took me some time, but I finally realized that my mouth doesn't always have to be moving. I don't always have to express my opinions—especially after Jim made a decision. Why speak thoughts I'll later regret?

Phase Two: Respond with a single positive word—After I was beginning to master saying nothing in Phase One, I graduated to Phase Two and started to respond with one positive word. I chose the word "Sure!" (and that's with an exclamation mark behind it and melody in my voice). And I began to use this positive response and say, "Sure!" on the small things.

My dear friend Dixie also chose the word, "Sure!" and let me tell you something that happened in her family as a result. Dixie's husband loved to go to Sam's Club, a crowded and noisy discount warehouse. Many times he would announce after dinner, "Hey, let's all go to Sam's Club!" Well, Dixie—with three

Once you've begun to respond positively to the small things, you'll quickly find it easier to respond positively to larger issues.

children, one of them a baby at the time—could have presented a watertight case against dragging the entire family out to Sam's Club on a school night after dark—but she didn't. She also never challenged Doug's leadership in front of her little family. Instead she just smiled, responded "Sure!" and got everyone into the car for another trip to Sam's Club.

Some years later as, one by one, Dixie's family members shared around the Thanksgiving dinner table about their favorite thing to do as a family, all three of her grownup children said, "Going to Sam's Club as a family!" Family unity, fun, and memories came because of Dixie's sweet heart—and word ("Sure!")—of submission.

Once you've begun to respond positively to the small things, you'll quickly find it becoming easier and even natural to respond positively to larger and larger issues—like car purchases, job changes, and household moves. I amazed myself one morning at 5:30 when the phone rang. Jim was calling from Singapore where he was traveling with our missions pastor. He didn't say, "Hello, how are you? How are the children? I miss you so much, I love you so much, and I can't wait to see you." No, instead he blurted, "Hey, how would you like to move to Singapore and minister?" And out of my mouth blooped "Sure!" followed by "Where is it?"

Maybe it was the early hour, or my loneliness for Jim, or the surprise...or maybe it was because in the preceding ten years I had grown in the area of following my husband. Whatever the reason, my training in responding positively paid off. God gave me the grace to say "Sure!" (And yes, we did go to Singapore and lived there for a year. It was a wonderful experience for our middle-school-aged daughters as well as for Jim and me. The four of us loved it so much we wanted to spend the rest of our lives there!)

Ask of each word, act, and attitude, "Am I bending or bucking?"—
Whenever tension wells up in your heart and you're resisting
or questioning your husband's direction, ask, "Am I bending or
bucking?" Your answer will point to the problem. Enough said.

Heart Response

Oh, dear one, don't let this look at God's guidelines for marriage be
a cold exercise. We are talking primarily about a *heart* response! Your
husband is your life mate. Whatever he is like, he is God's good and
perfect gift to you, part of God's plan for your personal fulfillment and,
more important, for your spiritual development. Your Christian character becomes evident each and every time you choose from your heart to
bend, to yield, to honor, to submit, to follow your husband. It's one way
that you, as a woman after God's own heart, honor God.

And what if you have a difficult husband? What if there are issues
where you aren't sure what to do? By all means, take advantage of the
wise people in your church—a pastor or counselor, a more seasoned
and experienced person, or a more spiritually mature woman (as in Titus
2:3-5).

And what if you have no husband? God gives each of us, His children,
a multitude of opportunities every day to develop a heart that considers
others. Out of honor for God, you can give preference to other people in
your life (Romans 12:10). Your dedication to honoring people honors God
and brings beauty to your life that reflects your heart after God.

7

A Heart That Loves

Part 1

*Admonish the young women
to love their husbands.*

TITUS 2:4

As I read along toward the end of the New Testament, little did I know that God had saved until last His most exciting insight about being a wife! In the tiny book of Titus, I discovered that *I am to hold my husband first in my heart after God.* That's the clear implication of God's instruction to the older women in the church who are to teach the younger women how to be women after God's heart. The first thing listed for married women to learn and practice is to love their husbands (Titus 2:3-4).

Heartfelt Yet Practical Love

When I looked at Titus 2:4 in my Bible, I thought, "Well, of course I love my husband!" But just to be sure about God's meaning, I made another trip to Jim's bookshelf. What I found on that blessed trip revealed another aspect of my job assignment from God. Let me explain.

God loves (*agapeo*) you and me unconditionally, regardless of our shortcomings, and certainly we wives are to love our husbands with that kind of unconditional love. But when God instructs us to "love" our husbands in Titus 2:4, the word is *phileo,* meaning *friendship* love—a love that cherishes, enjoys, and *likes* our husbands! Each of us is to value our husband and build a friendship with him.[1] We should see our husband as our best friend and want to be with him more than with any other person.

Yes, But How?

How can a wife nurture a heart of love, a heart prepared to support her husband in practical ways "until death us do part"?

Decide to make your husband your Number One human relationship—Our relationship with our husband is meant to be more important than the relationships we enjoy with our parents, friends, a good neighbor, a brother or sister, a best friend, and even our children—and the way we use our time should reflect that ranking.

I learned a lot about this kind of decision while reading a book written by a mother and her married daughter, Jill Briscoe and Judy Golz. Right before her daughter was married, Jill sat her down and told her that once she was married, she couldn't come running home and she was no longer to be dependent on her parents for anything.

Then the daughter wrote: "When [Greg and I] were first married, I almost automatically reached for the telephone whenever I had a certain problem or very good news to share. Usually before I finished dialing your number, Mom, I realized what I was doing, and I made sure Greg knew about it first before calling you."

Judy also asked her mother, "Do you remember the time Greg and I had a newly married tiff and I called you in tears? The first thing you said to me was, 'Judy, does Greg know you are calling me?'"[2]

I say, "Bravo!" to this mother who voluntarily stepped out of a Number One relationship with her daughter and showed her the way to make her husband her new Number One human relationship! After all, God said that we are to "leave and cleave"—to leave our parents and cleave to our mate (Genesis 2:24). When parents are overly involved in a child's marriage, problems can arise.

Your husband is to be Number One in your life (after God)—and he needs to know it. And everyone else needs to know it too.

In *Building a Great Marriage,* author Anne Ortlund suggests that couples consider signing an agreement that spells out the status between marriage partners and parents. She suggests the wording might go something like this: "I am no longer accountable to obey my parents. I am freed from that authority, to be bound, joyfully and securely, to my mate."[3] A pastor I know includes vows for the parents during the wedding ceremony: They basically vow to *stay out* of the new couple's marriage!

Whenever I counsel a young married woman, I enthusiastically encourage her to talk to her mother and mother-in-law about recipes, skills, crafts, interests, the Bible, and spiritual growth. But I am emphatic when I say not to talk to either woman about her husband. (And that works the other way, too. Mothers and mothers-in-law shouldn't be discussing their husbands with their daughters and daughters-in-law.)

To make your husband Number One will take some work as you deal with drop-in parents, learn not to plan things with either set of parents (or anyone else for that matter) without asking Mr. Number One first, and handle expectations ("Of course you'll be spending Christmas with us?…Or coming over every Sunday?… Or calling every day?"). Your husband is to be Number One in your life (after God)—and he needs to know it. And everyone else needs to know it too.

Begin to choose your husband over all other human relationships—Again, this includes your children. Two psychologists stated, "The point at which many marriages jump the track is in *over*-investing in children and *under*-investing in the marriage."[4] I read this true-life story to myself often.

"It's Too Late Now"

Today's letter will have a somber tone. I'm about to tell you a sad story…of a woman who put her children ahead of her husband….

These last two years he's been especially lonesome. Reason? His wife has literally latched onto their youngest daughter. She's one of those hang-on-to-your-children-for-dear-life mothers [and] this year when the last one enrolled at the university, she came unglued…. Now the lady is turning to her husband, hoping….

When was the last time they were close? He simply can't remember, and he can't forget the bitterness. All those years in second place he'd made a life of his own. Had to…. Not right. Of course it isn't. But…all these years his wife has been talking *to* him, *at* him, seldom *with* him…. Think of the fun they could be having now if they had developed a friendship.

I know too many men who, when their children came, turned down a lonesome road. And when you've gone too long single file, it's hard coming back to double. So much has happened alone it just seems easier to say, "It's too late now."…

You're wise to keep checking priorities…. You *can* be both mother and wife. But the wise woman remembers she will begin *and* end as a wife.[5]

Ask of your lifestyle, "Am I spoiling my husband rotten?"—This is what loving your husband is really all about—spoiling him rotten. And here are nine tried-and-true ways to groom yourself in the fine art of showering your husband with friendship love.

1. Pray for Your Husband Daily

The apostle James observed, "The effective, fervent prayer of a righteous man avails much" (James 5:16). Certainly the same is true of the prayers of a righteous wife for her husband. To pray for your husband efficiently and regularly, create a page for him in your journal. Write his name at the top, and then list the aspects of his life you want to faithfully hold up to God—his relationship with God, his spiritual growth both at home and in the church, any projects or deadlines on the job, his schedule for each day, his spiritual gifts, and his ministry involvement.

As you invest your time, your heart, and your life in prayer for your husband, you'll find arguments decreasing and mellowing.

If your husband is not a Christian, your primary prayer project is to beseech God to touch your dear one's life with His saving grace. Let the truth of God's Word be the substance of your prayers, truths like God is "not willing that any should perish" (2 Peter 3:9) and God "desires all men to be saved and to come to the knowledge of the truth" (1 Timothy 2:4). God's role is to save your husband. Your role is to pray fervently as you continue to love and serve him (1 Peter 3:1-6).

As you invest your time, your heart, and your life in prayer for your husband, you'll wake up one day and find arguments decreasing and a mellowing—even a warming—in your heart toward your husband. Truly, *it's impossible to hate or neglect a person you are praying for!*

Furthermore, Jesus teaches, "Where your treasure is [in this case, the treasure of your time and effort invested in prayer], there your heart will be also" (Matthew 6:21). Focusing on your husband in prayer will help you focus on him in your heart, your thoughts, and your actions. You'll also be surprised at the fruit born in your own life from this prayer—the fruit of understanding, cheerfulness, patience, helpfulness, and calmness. You'll realize that while you were praying for your husband, God changed *your* heart!

2. Plan for Your Husband Daily

It's a fact. Nothing just happens—including a great marriage! As much as you and I might desire to be wives who lovingly support their husbands, such loving support comes only with planning. As the Bible states, "Forethought and diligence are sure of profit" (Proverbs 21:5).[6] Here are some plans that will help you show your husband—and the watching world—that he is your highest human priority.

Plan special deeds of kindness—Each morning I ask God, "What is something I can do for Jim today that would help him, cheer him up, make him feel special, lighten his load?" Answers to that question include sewing on that missing button, running an errand for him, doing something on his "fix-it" list, even replacing old, worn-out socks with new ones. Let God be your guide.

Plan special dinners—This means dinners *he* likes. Take a lesson from Louise, a friend of mine who wrote from her new home in Oklahoma where her husband has his roots:

> One day I was cleaning out my recipe file at the kitchen table, putting all of my recipes into two piles—one to keep and one to throw away. Earl walked in and sat down at the table with me, picked up the pile closest to him and started sorting through them.
>
> "Oh, honey, I love this one!…And here's one of my favorites you haven't made in a long time…. Oh, I remember the night you made this one…. Hmmm, I wondered what happened to this one!" On and on Earl went.
>
> Elizabeth, he was going through the pile I was throwing out! I had made a decision to stop serving beef to my family. But now I've refiled all those "meat and potato" recipes and scheduled one night a week for the beef dishes.

Plan special times alone—And these times definitely have to be planned. In order to have special times alone with each other when the children were young, I scrimped and saved on our grocery budget so Jim and I could hire a babysitter each week for two hours. On our date we walked across the street to McDonald's, ordered two coffees (with unlimited refills), and, for a little more than a dollar, talked to our hearts content for two whole hours.

As the children grew older and their activities outside the home increased, Jim and I made a policy to *take advantage of any and all time alone*. It was easy to let special opportunities slip by unused, so we actively watched for chances to make our time alone a celebration of love.

While our children were growing up, Jim and I also planned a getaway for the two of us every three months—a practice we continue even with our empty nest. Those trips called for much research, saving, and planning (we traded babysitting with friends), but those priceless times were definitely worth the effort. We'd return 24 hours later refreshed and with a renewed commitment to each other and to our marriage.

Plan special dinners alone—Again, planning is key, and my neighbor Terri was a great model of this. Every Thursday she did "hot dog night" for her three boys. All week long she built up hot-dog night until the boys could hardly wait to eat them on Thursday—at 4:30! After devouring their yummy meal, they didn't even notice when they were whisked into the bathtub at 5:30. By 6:30 a story had been read, prayers said, and lights were out. Then out came Terri's linen tablecloth and napkins, two place settings of china, her sterling, and her crystal. She dropped a log into the fireplace and made a fire as a casserole emerged from the oven. Candles were lit, the lights turned down, and—voila!—a special dinner for two.

Plan an early bedtime for children—Plan to have your young children in bed early each night so that you'll have some quality time with your husband without competition from the kids.

An early bedtime is a practical way of choosing your husband's company over the distractions and interruptions of little ones. If you're avoiding these precious, cozy times alone with your husband, ask yourself why—and then remedy the situation.

Plan to go to bed at the same time—I know a night owl can be married to an early bird, but if it's at all possible, adjust your schedule to your husband's. Doing so will help make you a team, give you greater opportunities to help him get off to work each morning, keep the family on a schedule, and nurture physical love in your marriage. Again, planning is key.

As I said at the beginning of the chapter, we should see our husbands as our best friends, and we should work on building friendships with them. That work takes planning, but the rewards are definitely worth the effort as they flow out of a heart that loves.

Recently a wife told me that because her husband worked until almost midnight each evening, she was always asleep in bed when he arrived home from work. After all, she had her own job to rest up for. Well, she made the decision to set her alarm clock to go off in time for her to be slightly awake and "up" physically and mentally when her husband arrived home. She shared that when she announced her decision to her guy, she could see both joy and relief in his face and eyes. He couldn't believe it! And he was so happy. And, bonus of bonuses, it wasn't even a week before he asked her if she would share in couple devotions with him, something she had wanted for years.

You may not get this kind of response (and remember, you don't do things for your husband to *get* anything). But you will get an opportunity to be a couple, to visit, to prepare your husband a snack, and, if nothing else, to welcome him home with a smile and a hug.

Heart Pause

Why not pause and pray for your husband—your Number One friend—right now? Thank God for the love He has placed in your heart for your husband and ask for God's help in sharing it with your husband. After you say amen, do something special for your husband today that sends a message of friendship from your heart to his.

And then prepare your heart to discover in the next chapter even more ways to lavish love on him.

8

A Heart That Loves

Part 2

*Admonish the young women
to love their husbands.*
TITUS 2:4

What can you and I do to show our husbands affectionate, indulgent, friendship love? I promised you nine suggestions, and here are the rest of them. Whisper a prayer for your husband as you consider these ways to show him you care.

3. Prepare for Your Husband Daily

Preparing for your husband's homecoming each day shows him that he's a priority and communicates your heart of love.

Prepare the house—Take a few minutes before your husband is due home to pick up. Have the children help by putting away their toys. The goal is not perfection, but instead an impression of order and neatness. Many of my friends light scented candles, cut and arrange fresh flowers from the garden, turn on relaxing music, start a fire, and even pop something into the oven so their guys arrive home to a variety of sensations, which together communicate, "I'm glad you're home."

Obviously the opportunity for this step of preparation will come easier for a wife who's at home during part of the day or for a stay-at-home wife and mom. But even a working wife with a heart for her husband can think twice about how the house looks when she leaves it. After all, it's the first thing both she and her husband will see when they arrive home. It's amazing how much order can be achieved in five minutes by a woman working at full speed.

Prepare your appearance—If company were coming, you'd do a little something to freshen up, wouldn't you? Well, your husband—your Number One human priority—is far more important than company, so he should get the most special treatment of all. Run a comb through your hair, freshen your makeup, and change your clothes so he's not seeing the same old jogging outfit you had on when he left in the morning. Put on a bright color, a little lipstick, and a squirt of perfume (perfume rejoices the heart—Proverbs 27:9). After all, the most important person in your life is about to walk through the door.

Prepare the children too. In her classic book *What Is a Family?* Edith Schaeffer points out: "People so easily get annoyed with straggly looking children. It is good...to face the fact that the whole family will treat each other differently if they are dressed for the occasion, whatever that occasion may be."[1] Dirty faces, runny noses, hair hanging in the face don't make the best "Welcome Home!" Committee.

Prepare your greeting—You probably know approximately when your husband will get home from work each day. So warm his welcome as you wait and watch for him. If it's dark, for instance, turn on the porch light. In our home I watched out the front window until I saw Jim drive up. Then, prompted by my "Daddy's home!" the girls headed out the door with me to greet him.

Also be sure to plan your words of greeting. Your greeting will be more fruitful if you do. A good man ponders what to say (Proverbs 15:28), and "a good word makes [the heart] glad" (Proverbs 12:25). The moment of your husband's homecoming is not the time to ask, "Where have you been? Why are you so late? Why didn't you call? Did you pick up the milk?" It's also not the time to start listing the trials of your day. So ask God to give you just the right words—words that are positive and welcoming, words that focus on your husband and his frame of mind rather than yours. What you first say when your husband arrives home can set the tone for the entire evening.

Prepare the children to greet their father too. Be sure the TV is off. Give younger children a snack if it helps eliminate whining and grumpiness while they wait for Daddy—and for dinner. Learn from a darling cartoon I have of a mother and her two children standing in the family room with a checklist. Mom announces, "Your dad will be home any minute, let's go over the list: TV remote, check; comfy pillows, check; dinner, check; loyal canine companion, check; doting family, check!" How's your family doing in the doting department?

You can imagine my joyous surprise when Jim and I were visiting with one of my daughters and it was getting close to time for Dad to arrive home. It was dark, and it was late. But my daughter went into the living room, pushed the Off button on the TV, announced to her young children that Dad was only a few minutes away and she wanted everyone to give him a big greeting.

Furthermore she didn't want to hear the TV...or any bickering for the rest of the evening, that this was their dad's special time at home with his family. We *all* had a grand dinner and evening.

Set the table—Have dinner as close to ready as possible. Even if you haven't started the meal, a set table is the promise of what is to come.

"The king is in the castle!"—Countries with monarchs fly the royal flag over the palace when the king is in residence, and the hurry and scurry of servants' feet can be heard throughout the castle during his stay. Adopting this attitude and this approach (have your kids join you!) will help you pamper and love your king when he arrives home.

"The party!"—In an interview before Anne Bancroft's death, Hollywood couple Mel Brooks and Anne Bancroft discussed their then 40-year marriage. Anne specifically described her husband's homecoming. Each evening she would sit in her favorite chair and wait, listening for the sound of her husband's car, the crunch of its tires on the gravel driveway, the silencing of the engine, the slam of the car door, and the jingle of keys as he slipped one into the door lock. As the dead bolt slid open, she would grab the arms of her chair with both hands and think, "Oh boy! The party is about to begin!"

Now you and I aren't married to Mel Brooks, but we can both work on this kind of heart attitude. Like Anne, we can rejoice that the best part of the day has arrived—when our husband gets home and the party is about to begin!

Clear out all visitors—End your visiting well in advance of your husband's homecoming. He doesn't need to arrive home to a noisy houseful of moms and kids. After all, he's the king.

Stay off the phone—You're sure to hurt someone's feelings if you're on the phone when your husband walks through the door after work—either his feelings as you grimace and try to communicate with faces, sign language, and a weak wave or the feelings of the person on the other end of the phone line when you abruptly announce, "Oops, I have to go! My husband's home" and hang up. You know when your husband usually gets home, so set a cutoff time for making and receiving phone calls from friends.

As wives with a heart full of love for God and for the special husband He has given each of us, you and I are privileged to be able to prepare for his arrival home and to lavish our love on him. Do pour out God's love, which is poured out in your heart (Romans 5:5), when your husband walks through the door of his home. As Martin Luther said, "Let the wife make her husband glad to come home." Be sure he's not treated and greeted as the man who wrote the following words was!

The Homecoming

You know, when I get home after work, the only one who acts as if she cares at all is my little dog. She really is glad to see me and lets me know it.... I always come in the backdoor because Doris is in the kitchen about then.... But she always looks up from whatever she is doing with the most startled look, and says, "Oh, are you home already?"...Somehow she makes me feel like I've done the wrong thing just by getting home. I used to try and say hello to the kids, but I don't do that anymore. Seems I would get in between them and the TV set at just the wrong minute....So, now I just pick up little Suzy, my dog, stick her under my arm and go out in the yard. I act like I don't care, and maybe I shouldn't really—but I do. It gives me the feeling that all I am hanging around there for is just to pay the bills and keep the place up. You know, I believe that if the bills were taken care of and nothing broke, I bet I could be gone a whole week and nobody would even notice it.[2]

I know full well that in many marriages the wife arrives home after her husband, and maybe that's true for you. If so, what can you do to prepare for your husband?

Prepare all the way home—Put on some fresh lipstick and comb your hair. Use the trip home to plan those uplifting words of greeting—and then share them with a smile, a hug, and a kiss, of course! Plan to sit and snuggle a few minutes, if possible, and debrief the day's events. Have something in mind for dinner (or in the Crock Pot!), something simple and low-stress that will leave you more energy for your husband. Become an expert on quick, appealing meals. Even though you're tired, you can light candles, start a fire, and maybe even hum and laugh.

Pray all the way home—Prayer is the most important preparation of the heart. In prayer leave behind the events and people of your day and turn your heart toward home and your precious husband. Pray for your greeting, your words, your mealtime, your evening. Ask God for physical strength and energy. Relinquish any hopes and expectations of receiving help from your husband. If you get it, praise God—and your husband—profusely, but enter into your evening ready to give and expecting nothing in return (Luke 6:35). Reaffirm to God that your beloved husband is Number One, and ask for His joy in serving him.

4. Please Your Husband

If your husband is the king of the castle, you will surely delight in pleasing him. And pleasing him means paying careful attention to his wants, his likes, and his dislikes—and this takes a little doing.

What are your husband's likes? What are you doing in response to them?

My friend Gail is married to a sports nut so—after years of arguments over his habit of watching sports on TV every Saturday—she decided to join her husband in his particular "like." Gail purchased two Los Angeles Dodger T-shirts and baseball caps. As the game time neared on the next Saturday, she spread a red-and-white checked tablecloth on the floor in front of the TV, passed out the T-shirts and caps, and served a meal of foot-long Dodger dogs. Both of them had a ball at the ol' ball game!

Suzy, another friend of mine, had an even greater challenge when it came to pleasing her husband. Gary, a firefighter for the Los Angeles Fire Department, "liked" a farmer's breakfast of bacon, eggs, hash browns, and toast before he went to his job. So Suzy got up at 4:00 to fix him the breakfast he needed before he left for work at 5:00.

My Jim "likes" the salt and pepper shakers on the table. Monica's husband "likes" to read the paper in the morning before leaving for work. When Elaine's husband comes home to relax, he "dislikes" seeing toys strewn around the family room. Kathy's spouse "dislikes" the top of the refrigerator being dirty—something only he can see. What are your husband's likes and dislikes? And what are you doing in response to those?

5. Protect Your Time with Your Husband

You make your husband your Number One human priority when you protect your time with him instead of treating him as a built-in babysitter and darting out the door to shop when he gets home.

One wife and mother put it this way:

> This past week I made a small change in my weekly routine in order to put my husband as a priority. Generally I do my weekly grocery shopping in the evening, while my husband watches our two-year-old son. I've done this ever since my son became old enough to grab things in the basket. I felt that by shopping in the evening, I wouldn't have to look out for things rocketing from the basket and being squished and shaken. I could also be a whole lot quicker if I went by myself, thus conserving my time. Last week, though, I realized this probably wasn't the best use of my husband's time or of our evening, so I went shopping during the day. It didn't take that much longer, and my husband seemed to appreciate it.

Consider the following as a general principle, no matter how many decades you've been married: *If my husband is at home, I am at home.* My friend Debbie had to choose between time with her husband and time at our women's Bible study when his day off fell on the same day. Tom was understanding and supportive.

He said, "Go ahead, I'll make Wednesday morning my time to mow the lawn each week." So Debbie prayed…and chose time with Tom. Choosing to nurture her Number One human relationship, she has never attended Wednesday morning Bible study. Instead she goes to the Bible study offered on Wednesday night, when the entire family is at church for their various activities and commitments.

Being at home with your husband in the evenings is important too. It's easy to fill up your evenings with good things and miss out on enjoying the best thing—time with your man. One woman said she didn't know where her husband was every night. Then one night she stayed home—and there he was![3]

Ruth Graham is a wife who knows the value of protecting time with her husband. After a visit with Ruth at her home, an interviewer reported: "Everything is geared to Billy when he is in Montreat [their home]. Ruth refuses to have a firm schedule when Billy is there….The daily routine [is] carefully designed around her husband…."[4] A neighbor of the Grahams wrote, "Because Ruth is out of circulation when Billy comes home, her friends call him 'The Plague.'"[5] How's that for a goal?

6. Physically Love Your Husband

Read 1 Corinthians 7:3-5. A fundamental principle for marriage is "rendering affection" to one's mate. The Song of Solomon is a book of the Bible that details physical love in marriage. Proverbs 5:19 says our husbands are to be drunk with our sexual love.

I remember hearing God's view of physical love taught at a seminar I attended when I was a new Christian. I was so impressed (and convicted) I went straight home and announced to Jim that I was available to him physically at any and all times for the rest of our lives together! That may have been a slight overreaction, but I wanted to act on God's Word—and Jim got the message.

7. Positively Respond to Your Husband

We've discussed picking a positive word of response—a word or phrase like "Sure!" "Fine!" "No problem!" "Okeydokey!" "All right!" "Great!" "You bet!" "Anything for you, darling!" and "Cool!" (Notice the exclamation marks?) Imagine the lack of tension in a home where the husband's thoughts, decisions, and words are greeted so sweetly instead of met with resistance, negativism, or a lecture.

My simple but positive response meant no power struggle, no hurt feelings, no bitter words, no raised voices—and a much better start to our day.

Your immediate and gracious answer creates a nonthreatening atmosphere for communication and for asking questions—questions like "When would we consider doing that?" "How would we pay for something like that?" "What would this mean to the children?" and "Is there any other information we need?" Think of your response as being like a sandwich you're making. The first slice of bread—your initial response—is a positive, "Sure!" The items in between the bread (the meat, lettuce, tomatoes, etc.) are questions you ask for clarification, questions like those I just mentioned. The final slice of bread—your response of submission—is another positive "Sure!" Let me tell you about a sandwich I once made.

Early one morning while I was drying my hair with a blower, Jim asked if I could help him find something. My first (and fleshly) thought was "Can't you hear? I'm drying my hair!" A less selfish option—and a better one—was to yell above the noise of the blower, "Sure! I'll be right there as soon as I finish drying my hair." But God gave me the wisdom and grace to do the least selfish—and best—thing. I said, "Sure!" (the first slice of bread) as I turned off the blower. Then I asked my husband (here's the stuff between the two pieces of bread), "Do you need me to do that right now or is there time to finish drying my hair?" Even though I asked the question, I was ready to do whatever Jim said (the second slice of bread, the slice of submission). I stopped to communicate with Jim, indicating my willingness to serve. He had no problem with me finishing my hair, but the point was my readiness and desire to respond to him. My simple but positive response meant no power struggle, no hurt feelings, no bitter words, no raised voices—and a much better start to our day.

And just a note here. Sometimes the stuff between the two pieces of bread—the information gathering, processing, and discussing—can take time. It can require more than one conversation, even days or weeks as the two of you communicate. But the point is, you are more likely to be *able* to communicate when you are more positive to your husband's thoughts, dreams, and ideas.

8. Praise Your Husband

I have very few "nevers" in my life, but one primary "never" is never speak critically or negatively about my husband to anyone. I try instead to practice the wise advice a dear and godly saint at our church gave me in my wife-formative years. Loretta smiled and sweetly cooed to the group of younger wives I was in, "Ladies, never pass up an opportunity to bless your husband in public." (And, I would add, don't forget to bless him to his face as well!)

If you catch yourself speaking critically about your husband, quickly shut your mouth and do these three things:

- Search your heart. "Hatred stirs up strife, but love covers all sins" (Proverbs 10:12). Something is out of sync in your heart because "a heart of love draws a curtain of secrecy over the faults and failures of others....Love does not gossip."[6]

- Seek a solution. If some serious area in your husband's life needs attention, follow a better path than putting him down. Instead, devote yourself to prayer and, if you need to speak up, do so after much preparation and with gracious, edifying, sweet speech (Ephesians 4:29; Proverbs 16:21-24). You may also need to speak to a counselor, but remember that your time with a counselor is not for venting about your husband, but for getting help for *yourself* so you can properly deal with the problem.

- Set a goal. Make a resolution not to speak destructively about your husband but to bless him at every opportunity.

Blessing your husband in public—and in private—is one way to sow seeds of love for him in your heart.

9. Pray Always

We have come full circle. We began with prayer, and we end with prayer. A woman after God's own heart is a woman who prays. When does prayer make a difference? Try praying at these times.

- Before you speak in the morning
- Any time he is home
- Before he returns home
- Throughout the evening

- On the way to answer the phone (it could be him)
- When you are arriving home and he is already there

Take every opportunity throughout the day to ask God to enable you to be the kind of loving and supportive wife He wants you to be.

Heart Response

Surely the most important relationship in a married woman's life deserves her most focused attention. This chapter and the previous one have offered practical ideas from the Bible, books, my life, the experiences of other wives, and even the input from some husbands. To summarize, a wife who loves her husband is a wife who prays, plans, prepares, pleases, protects, physically loves, positively responds—and then prays some more. Put this whole list to work and you'll communicate "I love you" more powerfully than words alone can. And remember that a heart that loves is a heart that plans. So put on your thinking cap and begin the work of showing your husband the love that is in your heart!

9

A Heart That Values Being a Mother

Do not forsake your mother's teaching.
PROVERBS 1:8 NIV

"There is no greater place of ministry, position, or power than that of a mother."[1] I'm glad I didn't read these words when I first became a Christian. God had not yet taught me the truth of this statement, and I might have totally dismissed it. When Christ became the heart and soul of our home, I had two preschoolers, ages one-and-a-half and two-and-a-half. Katherine and Courtney were cute, but they had never been trained or disciplined. We had our moments of fun and shared some good times, but our home was generally filled with tension as I tried to coax and cajole and threaten them into acceptable behavior.

Even with my girls at such tender ages, I was absent from the home. Enrolled in a master's degree program in marriage and family counseling, I focused my time, my energy, and the effort of my heart on pursuing a counseling license to help *other* families—while I neglected my own. Farming out the children for long days spent with a variety of babysitters and different daycare centers, we had only to endure each miserable evening and weekend. The possibility of motherhood being a ministry or a place of great position and power was completely foreign to me.

But God—our ever-faithful God—opened my eyes and turned my thoughts about mothering around to His wise and perfect ways. When I first became a Christian, I sat in on a women's Bible study one night a week. There I began hearing things I had never heard before—comments about the "privilege" of being a mother, the awesome "responsibility" of raising children for God, and the "role" of the mother in training and discipling her little ones.

With the teacher continually pointing us to the Bible, I once again put that pink marker to the pages of Scripture, highlighting in my own Bible what spoke to me—this time as a mother. Studying these rosy highlightings, I discovered four passions that reflect a heart that values being a mother. We'll discuss two in this chapter and two in the next.

A Passion for Teaching God's Word

A woman after God's own heart is first and foremost a woman who has in her own heart a deep and abiding passion for God's Word. And her children—not the children at her church, not the women at her church, not her friends, her neighbors, or anyone else—are to receive the firstfruits of this burning personal passion. The Bible speaks at least twice of "the law" or teaching of the mother (Proverbs 1:8; 6:20), indicating that you and I as mothers are *on assignment from God to teach His Word to our children.* We as moms can do many things for our children, but teaching God's Word must be our passion. Why? Because God's Word (the Hebrew word *tora,* which means the divine law, the Word of God, the Bible) has value for salvation and value for eternity.

God uses His Word to draw people to Himself. The apostle Paul teaches that "faith comes by hearing, and hearing by *the word of God*" (Romans 10:17) and that "*the Holy Scriptures… are able to make you wise for salvation* through faith which is in Christ Jesus" (2 Timothy 3:15). Furthermore, God's Word never

> *We must have a passion for God's Word before we can share it with our children.*

returns to Him without first accomplishing His divine purposes (Isaiah 55:11). In light of this saving power of God's Word, we must place His Holy Scripture first on the list of things our children must know—and first in our own hearts! And it's obvious we must first have a passion for God's Word before we can share that passion with our children.

A Passion for Teaching God's Wisdom

Closely related to our call to teach God's Word to our children is our call to teach them His wisdom. In fact, the second meaning of the Hebrew word *tora* is wisdom. This definition encompasses principles, counsel, traditions, models of praise, guidelines for decision-making, and godly practices based on the Bible. Used in this sense, *tora* refers to practical and scriptural wisdom for daily life.

In Proverbs 31:1-9, we catch a glimpse of a mom who valued being a mother and treasured both her son and God's wisdom. In this chapter, her son King Lemuel records "the utterance which *his mother taught him*" (verse 1). Imagine the intimacy of the scene suggested here as a young prince perhaps sat at his mother's knee, absorbing—maybe even writing down—the words of wisdom his mother shared with him. He remembered her wisdom for the rest of his life, used it to guide his reign as king, and then passed it on at the end of the book of Proverbs. From her heart—to his heart—to your heart and mine!

Whenever I think of the calling to teach practical wisdom to my children, I think of salt. According to the Bible, my speech is to be "seasoned with salt" (Colossians 4:6), and this wonderful mothering verse gives me—and you—instruction, permission, responsibility, and encouragement to salt our children continually with God's wisdom. Out of our mouths at every opportunity must come salt—God's truth, words from the Bible, applications of the Bible's teachings, and references to God's presence with us and His sovereign power in the world.

In Deuteronomy 6:6-7, God says this to parents: "These words which I command you today shall be in your heart. You shall teach them diligently to your children, and shall *talk* of them when you sit in your house, when you walk by the way, when you lie down, and when you rise up." First a mother and father fill their own hearts with God's Word (verse 6) and then they deliberately and diligently teach their children at every opportunity each day presents (verse 7).

> *We need to talk about God to our children whether it's the "in" thing or not.*

When I discovered that I was on assignment from God to teach Katherine and Courtney God's Word and His wisdom—to season and preserve their lives with the salt of His truth—I had to train myself to be on tiptoe, ready and waiting for the opportunities that came as we sat and walked and drove through each day. I made the *decision* to be that ever-waiting, ever-watching mom, prepared to teach my daughters about God through the course of our everyday life.

I was helped along in my decision when I read that even the great evangelist Billy Graham had to choose to speak about the Lord. He realized he needed to create opportunities to share God's truth. So in the early days of his ministry and fame, he made a *decision* to mention the Lord every time he gave an autograph. He made a *decision* to turn every interview toward the gospel message. Writing to his wife Ruth, Billy reported, "I have decided in businessmen's luncheons to go all out for the Gospel. I am not going to give a talk on world events or give them sweet little lullabies."[2]

As mothers who want to raise children after God's own heart, we make a decision to "go all out for the Gospel" and relate every tiny thing to God. We need to talk about God with our children whether it's the "in" thing or not. After all, people talk about what is important to them, and when you and I talk about God, we communicate that God is supremely important to us. And let me remind you that you'll have more opportunities to talk about God's ways (and you'll be better heard!) if the TV is off— and that requires another decision.

Also, be aware that the practical wisdom of God is taught in two ways. The first is what we've been discussing, that we teach by our words, by our *talk*. But we also teach by our *walk*—by the way we live our lives. Our walk encompasses all that we do and say and all that we don't do and don't say. Our children are watching, and we are constantly teaching our children something, either positive or negative.

How's your walk? What are your children seeing about God in you? What are you teaching your children?

Yes, But How?

How does a mother who treasures her children, prizes God's Word, and values His wisdom go about teaching truth to her children?

Make some serious decisions—Discovering my mandate to teach the Bible to my daughters made me realize I needed to make several important decisions. Would I impart the Word of God to my two girls? Would I make time in our busy daily schedule for Bible teaching? And would I speak of the Lord continually? I knew that answering yes to these questions was dependent on yet another important decision—Would I reach over and turn off the TV (here we go again!) and pick up the Bible or a Bible storybook instead?

Whatever age the children are—16 days or 16 years—we must be teaching them about God and His Word in our homes. That privilege and responsibility is clearly part of our calling as women and moms after God's own heart. That kind of teaching needs to be part of the home we are building for God (Proverbs 14:1), a home that honors our Lord. Furthermore, this kind of teaching is exactly what our children need—whether they think so or not. You and I both know that we mothers give our children what they need, not what they want.

Recognize your role of teacher—Reading more about how Billy and Ruth Graham raised their children deepened my passion to impart God's Word to my own. When asked her opinions on her role as mother and homemaker, Ruth replied, "To me, it's the nicest, most rewarding job in the world, second in importance to none, not even preaching." Then she added, "Maybe it is preaching!"[3] Can you see your role of mother as that of preaching, of instructing and imparting biblical truth at every opportunity?

Consider these examples—As mothers on assignment from God, you and I cannot underestimate the urgency of planting His truth in our children's (or grandchildren's) hearts and minds early in life. What if the noble mothers of the Bible had missed their opportunities to sow the seeds of loving God in the hearts of their children?

- Jochebed had baby Moses with her for probably only three brief years before he went to live in Pharaoh's pagan household (Exodus 2). Yet this woman, who valued her role as a mother and was passionate about God and His truth, imparted enough of that truth to Moses in those few short years to help equip him to make serious choices for God later in life (Hebrews 11:24-29).

- Hannah faced a similar challenge. Like Jochebed, she only had her little Samuel for about the same three years before she delivered him at the doorstep of the house of the Lord to be raised by someone else (1 Samuel 1–2). And, like Jochebed, she taught her son enough of God's law to help equip him to become a powerful prophet, priest, and leader of God's people in the decades to follow.

- God chose Mary to raise His Son, Jesus, and she undoubtedly took seriously her assignment from God and daily poured God's rich truth into His little heart. Of course God chose the right home and the right mother for His precious Son, and by age 12 Jesus was amazing the teachers and scholars in the temple at Jerusalem with His knowledge. He was already going about His Father's business (Luke 2:46-49).

Are you sowing seeds of God's love and His truth in the hearts of your children? It's never too early or even too late to start—and something is better than nothing. So set a pattern, be sincere, and be consistent.

Memorize Scripture and read the Bible together—The biography of Corrie ten Boom, author, evangelist, and prisoner of the Germans during World War II, provides a more contemporary example of how a parent can pour God's Word into his children's hearts. Early in life, Corrie's father instilled in his family the importance of memorizing the Scriptures, and he saw that they learned Bible passages after their mother died. This memorization served his children well as they suffered and, with the exception of Corrie, eventually died for their faith. Corrie's storehouse of Scripture helped her survive the Nazi concentration camps. Her father told Corrie, "Girl, don't forget that every word you know by heart is a precious tool that [God] can use through you."[4] God's Word did indeed arm Corrie ten Boom and help her endure the pain and torment of the concentration camp. God also used His Word, hidden away in her heart, as a mighty instrument of evangelism right there in the camp as Corrie offered salvation, hope, and comfort to other suffering prisoners.

As important as memorizing Scripture is, we can't overlook the value of daily Bible reading. In addition to assisting his children in memorizing God's Word, Corrie's father read one chapter of the Old Testament to his family every morning after breakfast and one chapter of the New Testament every evening after dinner.

The parents of Elisabeth Elliot also took seriously their job of teaching God's truth to their children. Mrs. Elliot, whose first husband was savagely murdered on the mission field and whose second husband died after a long battle with cancer, testified to the value of her early training. She wrote, "In times of deep distress I have been sustained by the words of hymns learned in family prayers....Bible reading followed the hymn singing. My father believed in reading...*regularly* (twice a day aloud to us)."[5]

Missionary John Stam, martyred in China because of his faith, described daily life in his childhood home this way: "Three times every day, when the table was set for meals, Bibles were placed ready, one for each person. Before the food was served, prayer was offered, and then a chapter was read, each person taking part.... In that way, the Bible took first place in the daily intercourse of parents and children. It was the foundation, the common meeting-ground, the test and arbiter of all their thinking. It held and satisfied their hearts."[6]

Are you catching the vision—and passion—for God's assignment to pour His Word into the hearts of your children? The assignment never ends! When Elisabeth Elliot's husband Jim was killed, her mother wrote her a letter containing Scripture verse after Scripture verse. Even when Elisabeth was grown, raised, married, and a mother herself, her mother continued to pour God's Word into her heart.[7]

Follow the model of other mothers—God has allowed me to know a special family in which every member has a passion for His Word. When her first baby arrived, the mother decided to recite the Scriptures she was memorizing to her little ones each night as she tucked them into bed. One of her college-age daughters exclaimed to me, "Mrs. George, I don't even know how I learned so much Scripture by heart. I guess I've just heard my mother say it over my bed so often that I picked it up!"

This mother, who both valued being a mother and treasured God's Word, recited lengthy passages and even entire psalms and books of the Bible to her children at bedtime. When her son was playing basketball in

> *As mothers, you and I have countless, daily opportunities in our homes to plant God's Word deeply in the minds and souls of our children. We just need to take advantage of those opportunities.*

college, he made it a practice to go into the gymnasium before each game, lie down on a bleacher, and recite Romans 6 through 8 to calm his nerves and focus his heart on God. This son's fiancée told me that on her holiday visits to his home, this godly mother also tucked *her* into bed, reciting Scripture and praying with her—at age 22—as she made the rounds to all of her adult children's rooms. Another daughter, following in her mother's footsteps, told me how she and her husband returned home for Christmas and gave her mom the gift of a flawlessly memorized recitation of the book of 1 Peter. Her mother wept!

As mothers, you and I have countless, daily opportunities in our homes to plant God's Word deeply in the minds and souls of our children. We just need to take advantage of those opportunities. And we have the blessed privilege of tending their hearts and bringing them up in the training and admonition of the Lord (Ephesians 6:4). But first we must comprehend that the little (and once-little-and-now-big) hearts God has placed in our care as children and grandchildren are treasures indeed. Then we must nurture a heart of passion for His Word so that our passion will overflow into the lives of those we love.

Heart Response

As mothers, we cannot impart what we do not possess, so it is vital that you and I nurture a fierce passion for God's Word and wisdom in our own hearts. Do you treasure His truth, laying it up in your own heart (Psalm 119:11)? Do you spend time each day pouring it into your heart and mind—and into the hearts and minds of your children? Are you committed to giving God's Word a reigning position in your home and family life? What steps are you taking to ensure a regular time for teaching, reading, studying, discussing, memorizing, and even reciting the Bible?

10

A Heart That Prays Faithfully

What, my son?...And what, son of my vows?
PROVERBS 31:2

Have a goal

"Aim at nothing and you'll hit it every time." This saying fit my mothering like a glove before I found direction in God's Word. Up to that point I did nothing in our home to train my children. But once I found guidance, I moved ahead full steam. I took seriously my newly discovered and God-given "license to preach," and soon we as a family were poring over God's Word—and pouring it into our hearts. We picked verses to memorize together. Katherine and Courtney began having their own "quiet time" in addition to family devotions. And we all loved the wonderful Bible stories we shared at various times during the day. It was uplifting to center our home and our talk on God.

But my pink marker had another stop to make, this time at Proverbs 31:2—"What, my son? And what, son of my womb? And what, son of my vows?" These were the words of a mother, so they might have a message for me—but I couldn't begin to imagine what that might be. (What do *you* think this verse means?) In the end, this verse proved to be the most challenging aspect of my assignment from God, and the challenge continues to this day.

Well, I exhausted Jim's books and made a few trips to the seminary library before I began to understand the truth hidden in the verse and the message it had for me as a mother. I finally saw that this verse presents two more passions as it outlines my job assignment as a mom. First, this verse tells me that *I am on assignment from God to pray for my children.*

A Passion for Prayer

Proverbs 31:2 reveals a mother's anxious care for her child's good. He is the son of her vows, meaning a son she asked God for in prayer and dedicated to God (like Samuel in 1 Samuel 1). "Son of *my* vows" also suggests that her child was the object of *her* daily vows and prayers,[1] "a child of many prayers."[2] As one commentator noted, "Motherly training and dedication [provide]…the first imparting of religious instruction, the solemn dedication of her child to the service of God, [and] repeated and earnest prayer on his behalf. Her child is not only her offspring; he is 'the son of her vows,' the one on whom she has expended her most fervent piety."[3]

> *Each morning I asked God during my prayer time to touch my girls' hearts and open them to Jesus.*

How lovely is this image of a mother who thinks, loves, acts, speaks, and prays with a large and passionate heart! In her godliness she asks God for a child, dedicates that child to God, and then teaches him the ways of the Lord we discussed in the previous chapter.

But this mother's passion for God and for training her son in His ways doesn't stop with mere verbal instruction to the child. No, she also speaks *to God* on behalf of the child. The desires of her mother-heart go deeper and higher than basic teaching and training. She is a mother who prays, who expends her greatest efforts to nurture a righteous walk with her God *so that* she may effectively pray for her child. As a woman after God's own heart, she is vigilant about her own walk with God, dealing with sin in her own life (we're back to our first priority!) in preparation for entering God's holy presence and interceding for her beloved child.

Let me share how I began to live out God's daily (and lifelong) assignment of walking with Him and praying to Him. As a Christian mother (and like you, I'm sure), I desperately wanted my children to embrace the Savior I love. My highest aspiration was for Katherine and Courtney to become Christians—but that was something I couldn't make happen. Only God can do that. So I had no place to go but to God with this heartfelt desire for my girls.

Each morning when I woke up, I knew I would be asking God during my prayer time to touch my girls' hearts and open them to Jesus. I also knew that God's Word says, "If I regard iniquity in my heart, the Lord will not hear" (Psalm 66:18). I didn't want my sin and shortcomings to keep God from hearing my request for my daughters. No sin was worth its momentary pleasure when laid beside the eternal salvation of my children. I wanted something far greater than the brief pleasure that comes with speaking my mind, giving in to anger, and a multitude of other sins that might feel good for the moment. I wanted two souls for God!

Such is the mind-set of the godly mother of Proverbs 31:2 when she speaks of her child as "the son of her vows." And such is the mind-set you and I need to have regarding our own children.

We must be committed to nurturing and maintaining a godly life because a soul—the soul of each child—is involved. We gladly strive for a righteous walk—a righteous life—*so that* we can pray more effectively for our children!

Another thing I wanted for each of my daughters was a Christian husband, if they married. Again, because I couldn't choose for them, I once more turned to God with my fervent request. And rightly so. After all, my role was to be a mother who endeavored to walk with God, a mother who prayed fervently for her daughters to know God, to follow Him, and to be blessed with Christian husbands.

I'm sure these next statements are obvious, but I'll say them anyway. First, I did not pray for Katherine and Courtney every day—but my deep desire for their spiritual development was there every day (and still is). I carried my daughters with me in my heart every minute of every day, and I still do—along with their husbands and children.

Second, I have never walked through a day without sinning in some way. But because of my daughters and my desires for their walk with God (and my own walk with God, or course), I made the effort (and still do). I fought the battle against sin (and still do). I tried (and still try) to walk in a righteous way, according to God's standard and not the world's or my own. I took seriously (and still do) God's commands to put away sinful behaviors and to put on those that please Him and reflect Christ. All of these endeavors helped prepare me to pray on my children's behalf. And, besides training our children in God's Word and His ways (we'll get to that next), praying is all you and I can do!

Yes, But How?

How does a woman after God's heart foster a love for and a

commitment to praying for her children? How can you and I move toward fulfilling God's assignment to pray for our sons and daughters, grandsons and granddaughters?

Learn from godly and praying mothers and grandmothers—Real life examples will encourage you and model for you the role of prayers.

- Soon after his conversion, Billy Graham's mother set aside a period every day to pray solely for Billy and the calling she believed was his. She continued those prayers, never missing a day, for seven years until Billy was well on his way as a preacher and evangelist. His mother then based her prayers on 2 Timothy 2:15, asking that what he preached would meet with God's approval.[4]

- Leroy Eims of The Navigators' staff had a godly friend whose mother has prayed one hour each day for him since he was born.

- Jeanne Hendricks, wife of Dallas Theological Seminary professor Howard Hendricks, spent a season in intense prayer for one of her children. During his late adolescence, her son went through what Jeanne called a "blackout" period. He was unenthusiastic, moody, and depressed, communicating only with single-syllable responses. "This was one of the most traumatic times of my life," Jeanne admits. "He was so far from the Lord and from us. I felt like the devil himself was out to get my child. I prayed as I never had before."[5] I was present at a women's retreat where Mrs. Hendricks shared that during the half year when this situation continued, she covenanted with God to give up her noon meal. As she fasted each day, she prayed for her son for one hour until God broke through to him.

- Dr. and Mrs. James Dobson fast and pray for their children one day a week.

- Harry Ironside, former pastor of Moody Memorial Church in Chicago, had a mother who "never ceased to pray for his salvation. Throughout his life Harry would recall the substance of her pleas to God for him: 'Father, save my boy early. Keep him from ever desiring anything else than to live for Thee....O Father, make him willing to be kicked and cuffed, to suffer shame or anything else for Jesus' sake.'"[6]

Which model will you start following this week?

Ask God for His insights for your children—As you read about the remarkable mothers in the Bible and all their children accomplished for God, you can catch a glimpse of how God might work through your children. One of God's chosen mothers was Hannah, whose son, Samuel, began ministering for the Lord at a young age and later led God's people as prophet and priest (1 Samuel 3:1). The lovely and humble Elizabeth (Luke 1:60) helped nurture in her young son a love for God, and later his ministry as John the Baptist stirred people's passions when he preached and prepared the way of the Lord Jesus (Luke 3:4). And we never fail to be moved by Mary, the young woman who found favor with God (Luke 1:30) and was blessed among women (verse 28) to teach, train, and love her child, God's Son, our Lord Jesus Christ!

A Passion for Godly Training

As important as it is to *pray* for our children—for salvation and for Christian mates—we must not stop with prayer. We must also model a life dedicated to the Lord and train our children to follow His ways. Many times a woman starts off well—she gets married, wants a baby, prays for a baby, has a baby, and goes through a ceremony at church where she dedicates the baby to God. But then something happens—the baby becomes a reason for missing church.

Nancy, a young mother in my church, called me with a typical dilemma. It seemed that every time she put her baby into the church nursery he caught a cold. She knew the baby needed to be at church, she needed to be at church, and the family needed to be worshiping together, so she wondered what she could do. As we talked, she came up with a solution. She would take her baby into the church service and sit in the back row. If (or when!) the baby got fussy, Nancy would move out to the foyer where she could hear the message over an intercom system. If the baby still didn't calm down, she would walk around the church patio with her baby in the stroller. Nancy was so relieved that the entire family could go to church together again.

Our decision to take our children to church communicates to them—from birth on—the importance of worship and fellowship.

Another mom, married to one of our pastors, has sat in the foyer of her church through the baby and toddler stages of their three children. Each one of them has spent countless hours of pleasure at church crawling and climbing up and down the stairs leading to the church offices while Heidi listened to the sermons over the intercom. Those children have never known what it's like to *not* be at church on Sunday mornings.

Now this is not a lecture on rules about going to church, but I will say that attending worship faithfully instills an important habit in our children's lives and something into their hearts that nothing else can give them. Our decision to take our children to church communicates to them—from birth on—the importance of worship and fellowship in a corporate body (Hebrews 10:25). And this decision reaps untold dividends. For starters, your children will never know an option for Sunday.

Another reason to get your little (and big) ones to church is Sunday school. The teachers not only faithfully teach God's truth, but they also support at church what you are doing and teaching your children at home. These classes echo and therefore strengthen your messages about values, conduct, character, friendships, goals, and salvation through Christ—messages relevant to the important decisions children make as they grow up. Finally, whether you dedicated your children to God in your heart and prayers or in an official church ceremony, Sunday school is a practical way for you to live out that commitment.

Talk about church with eager anticipation all week long.

But getting there isn't easy. Believe me, I know! However, in most families the wife and mother (that's you and me!) is the key to getting the family to church on Sunday mornings. And what can you and I do to get our family off to church with more pleasure and less hassle? First of all, talk about church with eager anticipation all week long. Let your children see you looking forward to going to church. Also, begin preparations for Sunday on Saturday. Lay out the special church clothes for the next morning. Be sure baths are taken and hair is washed the night before and start preparing Sunday breakfast and lunch. One more thing—an early Saturday bedtime makes Sunday morning go more smoothly.

Another way we train our children in God's ways is to take

them—whatever their ages—to church for *maximum,* not just minimal, exposure to His people and their activities. Attend both church and church classes—and don't miss night church, if your church has an evening service. On Wednesday nights (or some other weeknight), many churches usually have something for children, youth groups for the junior high and high school students, and perhaps even activities for all ages. Getting your children involved is vital to training them up to know and serve God.

Granted, each opportunity in itself may not seem to offer much, but added up over a lifetime this frequent and regular exposure to God's Word and His people makes a powerful statement about our priorities and whom we serve. Getting our children to church for more than just the courtesy worship service visit (although even that can be a major accomplishment) is an essential part of training them in godliness.

When our two girls were growing up, we constantly reminded them that their priorities were family first, church second, and school third. Whenever there was a school event we told them, "That sounds like fun and maybe you can go, but if a special opportunity comes up for our family, or if a church activity conflicts with that school event, we're going to do that instead." Of course we attended a ton of school activities. And, of course, we encouraged our girls to bring their school friends to church activities. But Jim and I tried to apply "good, better, best" to our family activities, putting family first by taking them to church.

And of course getting them there meant driving! What mother isn't constantly driving her child to school, T-ball, basketball, football, soccer, swimming, ballet, gymnastics, shopping outings, and friends' homes (to name just some of the popular destinations)? We did most of the above, plus I added to all that activity by taking the girls to church too, to their youth group activities, and the homes of other church families—and it was wild…and wonderful!

On many Friday nights Jim and I would drop the girls off at the skating rink or bowling alley for an evening of activity with their church group and go to bed with the alarm clock set for midnight to wake us up in time to pick them up. Or, when the youth group had an all-night event at the church, we set the alarm for 6:30 (on a Saturday morning!) so we could pick them up at 7:00 when they were finished. These were definite sacrifices. And yes, it certainly would have been easier on us for the girls to stay home. But for us the end results (wholesome activities, safety, fun, exposure to God's Word, getting to know godly youth leaders and dedicated Christian kids, hearing the gospel, and getting to know Christ) far outweighed the inconveniences.

Heart Response

You and I will never know on this side of heaven all that our prayers accomplish on behalf of our children. Truly, the effectual, fervent prayer of a righteous mother avails much with God (James 5:16)! It is God's job to work in our children's hearts, but it is our job to make God's standards the standards of our own hearts and then to walk by those standards. Can you think of any area of your life that does not measure up to God's criteria? Where you are failing to follow Him? Once again, that's what this book is all about—becoming a woman after God's own heart. I hope and pray—for myself as well as for you—that we come to treasure God's Word, His wisdom, and His ways so that we can go boldly before His throne for our children's good (Hebrews 4:16)!

Also, the Bible tells us to examine ourselves. You and I need to do that often to, first, live a life that pleases God and, second, fuel our passion for godly training. God's kind of training takes time and dedication, and sometimes the passion needed for the long haul wanes. Ask your own heart, Am I committed to getting my children to church so they can be exposed to truth, no matter what it costs me? And am I committed to getting them there for maximum exposure to God, His truth, and His people—regardless of the personal sacrifice involved? Can you look ahead and envision the impact your faithful and regular decisions to train your children in godliness will have on them? It's never too late to shore up any weak areas in your heart or in your parenting. It all starts with you—and your heart after God! But thankfully it doesn't stop there. God is your willing and able partner as you raise your children to know Him and love Him and serve Him.

A Heart Overflowing with Motherly Affection

Part 1

Admonish the young women...
to love their children.

TITUS 2:4

As soon as I read God's instructions for Christian mothering, which we've been looking at, I began trying to follow them in our home. Chaos slowly became order, disobedience was being replaced by obedience, and structure began to emerge as we worked on keeping a daily schedule. But instead of feeling maternal, I felt like a drill sergeant, enforcer, and police officer all rolled into one. *Is this what a godly mother is?* I wondered. I knew in my heart that something was missing.

How I thank God that He showed me what that something was as I continued reading my Bible, eagerly searching for more verses on mothering. I found God's answer in Titus 2:4. There I read that mothers are "to love their children." On the surface, this

137

statement may not seem revolutionary, but when I (once again) borrowed my husband's books and dug into these four words, I found relief and freedom. I discovered that mothers are to be affectionate. They are to treat their children lovingly. In short, they are to be children-lovers.[1]

One more bit of information helped transform me from drill sergeant to a mother whose heart was overflowing with motherly affection. As we learned earlier when we discussed loving our husbands, the Greek language has several words for *love*. *Agapeo* is the kind of love God has for us as His children. He loves us in spite of our sin; He loves us unconditionally; and He loves us regardless and no matter what. And certainly we mothers are to extend this kind of godly love to our children.

> *I began to treasure Katherine and Courtney. They became people I wanted to be with, people I had fun with and played with, people whom God wanted to be my highest human priority after Jim.*

But *phileo* is the word God chose to convey mother-love here in Titus 2:4. *Phileo* love is affectionate love, a love that cherishes its object. It is friendship love, a love that enjoys children, a love that *likes* them! God calls parents to build the family on a foundation of biblical teaching, instruction, and discipline. The home gains a heart, however, when parents not only *love* their children but *like* them as well.

Our home certainly changed when I discovered God's call to enjoy my children. Oh, the praying and the training continued, but I let the party begin. God worked in my heart and changed me as I sought to follow His Word. I noticed that as I

Ephesians 4:32
Romans 12:9-12
2 Kings 22 - Josiah's tender heart

poured my life into the training and discipline and instruction God commanded, I began to treasure Katherine and Courtney. I saw my children as more than my duty. They became people I wanted to be with, people I had fun with and played with, people whom God wanted to be my highest human priority after Jim. Let me share some ideas for putting this kind of love into practice, the ten marks of motherly affection I strove to show for my two children...and now my seven grandchildren.

1. A Heart That Prays

The greatest gift of love you and I can give our children is to pray for them. For decades, I've believed the message of this anonymous poem I received as a new Christian:

> Some have had kings in their lineage,
> Some to whom honor was paid.
> Not blest of my ancestors—but,
> I have a mother who prays.
>
> I have a mother who prays for me
> And pleads with the Lord every day for me.
> Oh what a difference it makes for me—
> I have a mother who prays.
>
> Some have worldly success
> And trust in riches they've made—
> This is my surest asset,
> I have a mother who prays.
>
> My mother's prayers cannot save me,
> Only mine can avail;
> But mother introduced me to Someone—
> Someone who never could fail.

Oh yes…I have a mother who prays for me
And pleads with the Lord every day for me.
O what a difference it makes for me—
I have a mother who prays.

—Author unknown

Beginning each day by praying for your children benefits them in countless ways even as it draws them deeper into your heart.

2. A Heart That Provides

A heart overflowing with motherly affection lovingly and graciously provides the necessities of life for her precious family—nourishing food, clean clothing, and a safe home. Although we may not get too excited about running our homes on a schedule or cooking another meal or doing another load of laundry, a heart filled with motherly affection does just that. It puts self aside and loves the people in her home by caring for their physical needs. To fail to do so on a regular basis is neglect. (Neglect is defined by the U.S. Court system as *the deliberate failure to meet the physical…needs of a child*.)[2]

Many mothers wonder why their children act up, talk back, are grumpy, and require so much discipline. Maybe it's because Mom isn't providing the basics of nutritious, scheduled meals, clean bodies, clean clothes, and adequate sleep and rest.

3. A Heart That Is Happy

When our children (and our husbands!) can count on us to be happy, home life and family relationships take a leap toward heaven. Whether the alarm has just gone off in the morning, or you're picking the children up from school, or they're walking in the door after their own activities, they need to know that

A thankful heart produces a happy heart (celebrating, fun, etc.)

Romans 1:21 - not thankful leads to a darkened heart

you will be happy. I decided to work on the habit of happiness when I read Psalm 113:9 (another verse I marked in pink): "He [makes] the barren woman to keep house, and to be a *joyful* mother of children."[3]

So I began to pray—a lot! I would pray when I heard my girls' first little waking up sounds and walked toward their rooms. In later years I prayed as I went to pick them up from school. I wanted them to see that I was excited about being with them after they had been gone all day at school. (As Elisabeth Elliot said at a seminar I attended, "You create the atmosphere of the home with your attitudes." I kept that in mind!)

> *As mothers, we are the Number One influence in our children's lives.*

I also learned to "light up" after reading this personal account written by a son about his father. *Psalm 126:3*

> Something about my father attracted me like a magnet. When school was out, many times I would rush to his hardware store instead of going out with my friends. What drew me to my father? Why did I prefer a visit with him over some of my favorite activities? As soon as I set foot in his store, it seemed as if his whole personality lit up. His eyes sparkled, his smile gleamed, and his facial expressions immediately conveyed how glad he was to see me. I almost expected him to announce, "Look, everybody, my son is here." I loved it. Although I didn't realize it at the time, those tremendously powerful nonverbal expressions were the magnets that drew me to him. Ninety-three percent of our communication is nonverbal....Whenever you see [your child],

Colossians 3:16-17 - giving thanks to God admonish one another

Prov. 15:13, 15, 17:22 - merry heart (happy)

"light up" with enthusiasm, especially in your facial expressions and tone of voice. That light comes from the inner knowledge that he's valuable.[4]

As mothers, you and I are the Number One influence in our children's lives. We have the privilege of "lighting up" when we see them and sharing with them the happiness that is in our hearts. And that happiness is wonderfully contagious.

4. A Heart That Gives

The Bible is full of exhortations for Christians to be about the business of giving. As we've seen several times already, that's how our Savior lived. Mark reports, "For even the Son of Man did not come to be served, but to serve, and to give His life a ransom for many" (Mark 10:45). Here are a few principles that can help us be mothers who give, mothers who serve—and who do so with affection, warmth, and energy.

Give because it is your role—Because of who God is, a woman after His heart is a woman who gives. As Christians we are to give, as wives we are to give, as mothers we are to give, as singles we are to give, as members of a church body we are to give. That's our role, our assignment from God, as His children. We give the smile, the cheerful greeting, the hug, the compliment, the encouragement, the praise, the meal, the time, the listening ear, the ride... and the list goes on and on.

As Edith Schaeffer points out in every chapter of *What Is a Family?*[5] *someone* has to create family memories and undertake the wondrous task of having the family become a work of art. Someone has to be the nest maker and interior decorator. Someone has to take time to pray and plan surprises. Someone must see the family as worth fighting for, worth calling a career, worth the hard work of training a child in godliness, worth the relentless tasks involved in running a home. On and on Mrs. Schaeffer writes, showing the reader that this "someone" is the wife, the mom, and the homemaker and that, as such, she must embrace a life of being the giver. That's our role as mothers.

Give generously—Take heed of these two sowing and reaping passages from the New Testament (only the pronouns are changed!): "She who sows sparingly will also reap sparingly, and she who sows bountifully will also reap bountifully" (2 Corinthians 9:6) and "Whatever a [mother] sows, that she will also reap" (Galatians 6:7). As I considered the principle of sowing and reaping, I realized that, in a general way, what I put into my children on a daily basis—seeds of patience or impatience, faith in God or lack of faith, kindness or selfishness—would be what I might gain back in years to come.

Give expecting nothing in return—Even as we consider the principle of sowing and reaping, we must remember that mothers are to have no ulterior or selfish motives when it comes to giving. We serve and take care of our children simply because God says to. Just as we do for our husbands, we give to our children expecting nothing in return. We don't give motherly love in order to receive praise, thanks, recognition, or good behavior. (Those things may never come.) No, we give our love in a myriad of practical forms simply because God expects that of mothers. There are no other options, no conditions, no exceptions, and no fine print when it comes to God's clear command that we are to love our children (Titus 2:4).

5. A Heart of Fun

Living in your home should be an absolute ball for every family member. To make that true in my home, I worked on developing and using a sense of humor. I learned to smile and laugh—a lot.

I checked out silly riddle books from the library every week, and my girls and I laughed and rolled on the floor as we read them.

Most of all, I began to freely use the words "I love." I used that phrase to point out the good of every aspect of our lives: "I love Saturdays…the Lord's Day…Wednesday nights at church… having your friends over…our evening dinners together…our family devotions…praying with you…praying for you…going for a walk with you…sitting around and listening to music together.

> *Let the meal be a time for physical refreshment and pleasant fellowship.*

I love everything—and especially I love you!" I still say "I love you" to Katherine and Courtney— now grown and married and moms themselves—(and Jim, too, of course) every time I see them, or tell them goodbye, or talk to them on the phone.

Also, to have a happy home, be sure to make mealtime fun. We can learn a lesson from how and when our resurrected Lord spoke to Peter, the disciple who had three times denied knowing Him. Rather than confronting Peter before or during the meal, Jesus *waited until after* the meal. He let the meal be a time for physical refreshment and pleasant fellowship (John 21:15). Are we doing the same in our homes?

Heart Pause

We're halfway through the ten marks of motherly affection. Are you catching a vision for God's plan for your relationships with your children and for how to lavish love on them? As God's mothers, we pray, provide, and play. Pause now and ask God to fill your heart with more love for your children—with love that prays for and takes care of our children, a love that teaches and trains, and a love that laughs and plays.

12

A Heart Overflowing with Motherly Affection

Part 2

Admonish the young women...
to love their children.

TITUS 2:4

God's assignment to mothers can sound overwhelming if we don't remember that through His Word, in His power, and by His grace He fully provides all that we need to do what He commands. What a privilege to care for the children He blesses us with and to raise them for His purposes! Now for a few more marks of motherly affection.

6. A Heart That Celebrates

Another principle I took to heart from God's Word is the "extra mile" principle. Our Lord teaches, "Whoever compels you to go one mile, go with him two" (Matthew 5:41). Let's face it, we *have* to be mothers, and we *have* to do the duties. That's the first mile of our job assignment from God. So...why not go the extra mile and make everything you do special? Why not turn the mundane into a celebration?

Take, for instance, the evening meal. We *have* to have dinner—so why not make it special? Simply light a candle, find a flower or some interesting greenery in the yard, use seasonal decorations, change tablecloths and placemats, or use special dishes. My daughters loved the few odds and ends of a stoneware pattern with rose clusters and gold edges that I picked up at a garage sale. My friend Judy purchased a red plate with gold lettering around the edge reading, "You are special today." Whenever she senses that someone in her family is down or going through tough times, she prepares her "Red Plate Special," setting the hurting member's place at the table with that bright plate.

Or you can eat in special places—and I don't mean a restaurant! Use your patio. Pack a picnic. Eat cross-legged on the floor in a different room. Be creative not only about where you eat but also about what you eat when. Serve a "backwards dinner" and start with dessert. Or number the different parts of the meal, have each person draw a number, and then serve dinner in the order the numbers were drawn! Or make dinner a treasure hunt with clues leading to each item on the menu—some hidden inside the house and some outside. You can go the extra mile toward fun and celebration with very little effort.

And why not make your church day the most special day of the week? Ruth Graham "made Sunday the best day of the week. There was always some kind of shared activity or outing in the afternoon and the children were given treats....It was the Lord's day, a day to rejoice and be grateful."[1] Do whatever you need to do to go the extra mile and celebrate being Christians.

Finally, if someone is sick, bring out the "sick tray" and serve meals on it with a flower, a candle, a few stickers, and special dishes. And don't forget to put the "sick bell" by the person's bed. Let your patient ring it anytime for anything! The mundane tasks of daily life—the first mile—are great opportunities for celebrating the extra mile.

7. A Heart That Gives Preferential Treatment

Titus 2:4 teaches us that our husbands and children are to take priority over all other human relationships and responsibilities. That's why I developed this principle to guide the motherly affection of my heart: *Don't give away to others what you have not first given away at home.* And let me tell you how this principle was born.

Late one afternoon I was hurrying my two little girls into the car so we could deliver a meal to "Mrs. X" who had just had a baby. All day long I'd labored on the meal for this woman who needed the help of people in the church, a woman I didn't even know. I had baked a pink, juicy ham, created a pressed Jell-O salad in a pretty mold, steamed brightly colored vegetables, and topped it all off with my most special dessert. As we started out the front door, Katherine and Courtney wanted to know who the food was for. I lowered the beautifully arranged tray to their level and took advantage of this opportunity to teach them about Christian giving. I explained, "Mrs. X has had a baby, and we're taking dinner to her family so she can rest after being in the hospital."

That sounded good until my own children asked, "What are we having for dinner?" When I

Is there a difference in the tone of your voice you reserve for your friends and the one you use with your family?

said that we were having macaroni and cheese with hot dogs (again!), I was sharply convicted of my wrong priorities. I had put someone else, Mrs. X, ahead of my own family. I had gone *many* extra miles to make the meal I was taking to someone I had never met, but I was throwing together something quick and easy for my own husband and children. In short, I was giving something to someone else that I had not first given to the people closest to me!

Since that moment, I have made the same meal for those at home—people light years more precious to me than anyone else ever will be—that I make when I do a good deed. And when I take a dish to a potluck, I make two of them. When I take a dessert for some gathering, I take it with two or three pieces missing—pieces left behind for my VIPs.

This principle—*Don't give away to others what you have not first given away at home*—applies to far more than just food. We talk to people on the phone, for instance, but we don't talk to our own children. We listen to other people, but we don't listen to our children. We spend time with other people, but we don't with our children. We give smiles and joy to others, but don't always share these with our children.

One mother asked, "Have you ever noticed a difference in the tone of voice you reserve for your friends and the one you use with your family? It's so easy to give our best to comparative strangers and toss our families the leftovers." She then went on to report, "One young mother of eight children came into the family room and found all her children bickering. She gently admonished them, 'Children, don't you know the Bible says we should be kind to one another?' Her oldest, who was nine, looked thoughtfully around the room and replied, 'But, Mommy, there's nobody here but the family!' "[2]

8. A Heart That Is Focused

When I read Jesus' words that "no one can serve two masters" (Matthew 6:24), another mothering axiom was born: *Beware of double booking.* By "double booking," I mean trying to focus on our children and other people at the same time. Here's an example of double booking.

Once I was counseling a mother on the phone about the rocky relationship she had with her teenage daughter. We had talked well over 20 minutes when I heard her say, "Oh, hello, honey." When I asked, "Is someone there?" this mother said coolly, "Oh, it's only my daughter." It was 3:30 in the afternoon. This daughter—this *"only my daughter"*—had left in the dark at 7:00 that morning. The mother hadn't seen her daughter for more than eight hours, and all her daughter got was, "Oh, hello, honey"— a clear case of double booking. This mom had clearly double booked by being on the phone with me (this time I was Mrs. X!) when she knew her daughter—the one she was having problems with—was about to come home. She sent a message to both of us that, at that moment, I was more important than her God-given daughter.

> *She was not about to lose one second of her precious time with her daughter by having us there.*

Now let me tell you about another mother whom my friend Beverly and I both admired as a Christian, a wife, and a mother. When we called to schedule a get-together, she invited us to a lovely lunch that we enjoyed in her breakfast room. From our table inside, however, we could see another table outside on her patio—a table set with linen placemats, starched linen napkins, freshly cut flowers in a vase, two sterling silver spoons, two crystal plates, and two crystal goblets for ice water. That lovely table had been set in honor of *her* teenage daughter's much-anticipated arrival home from school. This thoughtful, loving mom had two more desserts in long-stemmed crystal glasses waiting in the refrigerator—and she did something like this *every* day! (On those days when she had to be gone when her daughter came home, she left a love note on a set table and a special treat in the refrigerator.)

At 2:30, this wise mother—a mother who understood her priorities and watched the time—began to shoo the two of us out the door because someone more special was coming! She graciously said, "Well, I'm sorry we have to end this, but I'm expecting my daughter home in 15 minutes, and that's our special time." She was not about to lose one second of her precious time with her daughter by double booking and having us there. She had given us the gift of time—rich, life-changing time for Beverly and me—but our hostess truly lived out her priorities. She knew where to focus her efforts. (When we left, I barely had time to rush home and throw some placemats and granola bars on the table before Katherine and Courtney came home in the car pool. But I also knew all future welcome home snack times would be a *little* more special.)

9. A Heart That Is Present

Our presence in the home is important. No dollar amount can ever be put on the value of our presence at home after school, in the evening, at night, and on weekends and holidays. No Tupperware party, crystal party, or plant party with the girlfriends can compare to sharing dinner with your family, helping your kids get ready for bed, tucking them in, reading to them, praying with them, and kissing them good night. *Nothing* can compare!

When I was invited to participate in a certain ministry opportunity, I asked my daughters their thoughts on my involvement. I wanted them to *know* they held the premiere place in my heart and were more important to me than other people or activities. Then, having received my husband's okay and my children's blessing, I accepted the ministry opportunity, knowing all was well at home. I had my family's full support. They wanted me to minister and were at home praying for me. Only once in 25 years of mothering did one daughter (a sixth grader at the time) say, "I wish you didn't have to go." We had just arrived back from the mission field, were settling back into a school routine, and I had thrown myself back into church activities. Well, that's all she had to say to let me know I was needed at home. I had overestimated her stability and underestimated the time it would take to adjust our way back into our culture.

10. A Heart That Is Quiet

Remember how we learned not to talk about our husbands? That same principle applies to the children too. The Proverbs 31 mother offers us a lesson about quietness. We learn that "she opens her mouth with wisdom, and on her tongue is the law of kindness" (verse 26). Words from this lovely mother's lips are marked by wisdom and kindness, and neither of these qualities promote talking about her children in a negative way. After all, "love covers all sins" (Proverbs 10:12). A loving mother whose heart is quiet never broadcasts any harmful or critical information, not anything general and nothing specific, about her children. A friend of mine communicated volumes about her home life (and her heart) every time she warned younger moms in quite general terms, "Just you wait. Having teenagers is awful!"

How I thank God for Betty, a sharp contrast to my friend. Betty never failed to speak positively and enthusiastically about her child-raising years. She would ask me, "How old are the girls now?" When I answered, "Nine and ten," she exclaimed, "Oh, I remember when my boys were nine and ten. Those are wonderful years!" Years later when my answer to her same question was "thirteen and fourteen," Betty again cried out, "Oh, I remember when my boys were thirteen and fourteen. Those were wonderful years!" No matter what age Katherine and Courtney were, Betty saw them as wonderful years. Oh, I'm sure she encountered the usual challenges, but Betty was a mother whose heart was filled with motherly affection for her boys, whose home was filled with fun, whose heart was positive about God's job assignment for her—and whose lips were respectfully quiet about any difficulties.

God's solution for the challenges we face raising children (the children He gave us and the challenges He knows we face as we train them up) is the "older women" of Titus 2:3. So I encourage you to develop a relationship with an "older woman" like Betty who can help and encourage you. Talk to her—and to God—about mothering. Ask her and the Lord your questions about how to fulfill that awesome responsibility and blessed privilege with a heart of affection for her children.

Heart Response

We've come on quite a journey through Scripture as we've learned about being God's kind of mom. How blessed we are to pray for our dear children. What a challenge to train them in God's ways. And what a delight to set the tone in the home—a tone of love and laughter and fun. Is yours a heart filled with motherly affection? Do you cherish your children—and do they know you do? Do you enjoy your family and look forward to spending time with them? Being the kind of mother who pleases God calls for prayer. After all, He is the one who makes our hearts joyful, generous, giving, happy, and quiet. He enables us to focus on and live out our priorities. And He provides what we need to go the extra mile and mother our children the way He wants us to. The job assignment isn't easy, but we can do all these things through Christ who strengthens us (Philippians 4:13)!

MARK 9: 36·37
35

13

A Heart That Makes a House a Home

The wise woman builds her house.
PROVERBS 14:1

One evening at bedtime, right before I turned off my light, I read this lovely description of a home written by Peter Marshall, former chaplain of the United States Senate. Maybe it will open your eyes and touch your heart as it did mine.

> I was privileged, in the spring, to visit in a home that was to me—and I am sure to the occupants— a little bit of Heaven. There was beauty there. There was a keen appreciation of the finer things of life, and an atmosphere in which it was impossible to keep from thinking of God.
>
> The room was bright and white and clean, as well as cozy. There were many windows. Flowers were blooming in pots and vases, adding their

> fragrance and beauty. Books lined one wall—good
> books—inspiring and instructive—good books—
> good friends. Three bird cages hung in the bright-
> ness and color of this beautiful sanctuary, and the
> songsters voiced their appreciation by singing as if
> their little throats would burst.
>
> Nature's music, nature's beauty—nature's peace....
> It seemed to me a kind of Paradise that had wandered
> down, an enchanted oasis—home.[1]

What hit me—aside from the beauty of this image—was the realization that my home (and yours) can be a little bit of heaven, a kind of paradise, to my dear family and to all who enter its sanctuary. As I fell asleep that night, I dreamed about making my house a home in which it was impossible to keep from thinking of God.

But when reality set in the next morning with the squawk of my alarm clock, I knew dream time was over. It was time to go to work if I was going to make my dream come true. *But how?* was the urgent question on my mind. And once again God's perfect Word came to my rescue with His answers.

The Business of Building

Proverbs 14:1 reads, "The wise woman builds her house." Needing building instructions for making my house a home, I took this verse apart, starting with the positive aspect of building. "To build" means, literally, to make and to set up a house[2]— and this verse refers not only to the structure and upkeep of the home, but also to the family itself. You see, a home is not only a place—it's also people! One insightful scholar explains the verse this way:

Although the Hebrew word for "house" and "home" is the same, "home" is the preferred word here. A house is not always a home and this verse does not speak of house construction, masonry, or carpentry but of home building; the knitting together of family and the day-by-day routine of creating a happy and comfortable place for a family to live.[3]

And who is responsible for the quality of life in that place where the family lives? The woman! She sets the mood and maintains the atmosphere inside the home. In fact, this proverb teaches that if the woman is wise, she diligently and purposefully creates that atmosphere. She doesn't just hope it will happen.

Creating the atmosphere—Creating the atmosphere of a home is very much like using your thermostat to regulate the temperature inside your house. You decide on an ideal temperature for your family and set the dial to a comfortable level. Then the thermostat takes over and goes to work maintaining the desired temperature. If the house starts to get hot, the thermostat automatically turns on cold air to cool it off. If cold air moves in, the thermostat receives the signal and gets busy warming up the house.

> *God gives us the heart, the wisdom, and the words to create a healthy atmosphere.*

Well, I've discovered that in my home *I* am the thermostat. I want the atmosphere inside our house to be warm, cheerful, loving, positive, and constructive. So I try to go to God's Word each morning and pray, giving Him the opportunity to set the temperature of my heart to match His. Then I go to work to maintain the comfort in my home. If things start to get hot (hot words, hot tempers, hot emotions), I set about to bring in cooling, soothing words ("a soft answer turns away wrath"—Proverbs 15:1) and words of peace ("the fruit of righteousness is sown in peace by those who make peace"—James 3:18).

Likewise, if things start to cool off (cold hearts, cold feet, cold shoulders), I go to work giving a good word that makes hearts glad (Proverbs 12:25), remembering that "a merry heart makes a cheerful countenance" (Proverbs 15:13) and that "he who is of a merry heart has a continual feast" (Proverbs 15:15). Such times are a challenge, but as I seek to live God's way and look to Him for the grace to do so, He gives me the heart, the wisdom, and the words to create a healthy atmosphere. He will do the same for you as you build the atmosphere of your home.

Building a refuge—As the center of family life, the home ministers to our family far more than we might imagine. I remember a time my husband made this fact very clear. He'd had "one of those days" that had stretched him to his absolute limit. A seminary student at the time, Jim had left the church parking lot at 5:00 in the morning to attend classes and deliver his senior sermon. After his commute back to the church through downtown Los Angeles traffic, he had officiated at a funeral and graveside service for a woman who, having no one to help bury her husband, had called the church the day Jim was "pastor of the day." All of this was topped off with a late meeting at church.

> *What a blessing if every member of your family and mine knows home is the one place on earth where everything will be all right.*

I had the porch light on and was watching out the kitchen window as I waited—and waited up—for Jim. When he finally got to the front door, he didn't walk in—he sort of slumped in.

On the way in, my exhausted husband sighed, "Oh, Liz, all day long I kept telling myself, 'If I can just get home, everything will be all right.'"

"If I can just get home, everything will be all right." What a blessing it would be if every member of your family and mine knew that there is one place on earth where everything will be all right! Home would truly be a wonderful haven and refuge for them, a "hospital," as Edith Schaeffer says.[4] And what a worthwhile goal for us—to build the kind of home which strengthens and renews each family member. Mrs. Dwight Eisenhower had that goal for her famous husband and president of the United States. She wanted to build a "home [where] he belonged to her world, a world of lighthearted family life where there were no pressures."[5] Imagine such a refuge!

Our children as well as our husbands benefit from our building efforts. One counselor reported that "a secure home life tends to reduce frustration and uneasiness in a child's life, and it gives them the ability to cope with pressures more effectively."[6] And that's only one advantage that we give our children when we go about the business of building a home.

What is true about the importance of a home in life is also true as the end of life nears. When terminal cancer forced Bible scholar and author Dr. Francis Schaeffer to leave his beloved L'Abri in Switzerland and live in America where he could receive the best treatment, his wife's first concern was to establish a home. When she was asked, "Why a 'home'?" Edith said she would answer that "home is important to a person to help him or her get well, as well as being important for family times together if someone is dying. In either case, beauty and familiar surroundings have an effect on the physical, psychological, and even spiritual state."[7] What a worthwhile building project—making our home a refuge for our family. Even the word "refuge" brings a calmness to heart and soul.

Avoiding the negatives—"Every wise woman builds her house," Proverbs 14:1 begins, but the second half is just as important—"the foolish [woman] pulls it down with [her] hands." To pull down a home means to break or destroy it, to beat or break it down—to ruin it.[8] How can a woman pull down her own home? How can she be a one-woman demolition machine? My own experience offers two answers to that question.

First, a woman can cause great damage actively—by working destruction. What, for instance, does anger out of control do? It throws, it slams, it tears, and it rips. It also breaks things as well as rules. As if *doing* these destructive deeds weren't bad enough, anger out of control also *speaks words* that break, destroy, ruin, and kill.

Molly Wesley, the wife of Methodism's founder John Wesley, must have been a woman who pulled down her home. Her husband wrote her a letter listing ten major complaints including "stealing from his bureau, his inability to invite friends in for tea, her making him feel like a prisoner in his own house, his having to give an account to [her] of everywhere he went, showing his private papers and letters without his permission, her use of fishwife's language against the servants, and her malicious slander."[9] These are sure ways to pull down a home!

The second way to ruin a home is passive—by simply failing to work. We can slowly erode the foundation of our home by our laziness, by simply "never getting around to it" (whatever "it" may be), by neglect, by forgetting to pay a bill...or two, by successfully putting things off, by not spending enough time at home. Then there's the problem of too much—too much TV, too much reading, too much shopping, too much time with friends, too much time spent on the phone or internet.

I know that your heart is intent on following after God's heart and His ways. That's why you're reading this book. So I am certain you want to make your house into a home. Having that heart desire is an important step. Making a house a home is indeed a matter of the heart.

Yes, But How?

How does a woman who desires in her heart to make a house a home carry out the building process? What can we do to be used by God to create the kind of place He has in mind for our families?

Understand that wisdom builds—The wise woman is aware that she's on assignment from God and knows that building a home is a lifelong endeavor. The teaching of the Bible is clear, and so is the sharp contrast between the wise woman and the foolish woman. Wisdom builds—and builds and builds—avoiding any attitude or act that doesn't build. And this kind of building effort is wise whether you're building a home for yourself or for a husband and children. Let me explain.

When my two daughters were growing up—when they were preschoolers and when they were career women living at home and every step in between—they were building their own room, which was their "little house." I used a 3" x 5" card system for work chores, with a set for me and a set for each of them. When I cleaned the house, Katherine and Courtney each cleaned their room. While I dusted, they dusted—and on and on their cards went, matching mine task for task. They each had their own dirty clothes basket and, from the time they could climb up on their

Tommie Tippie, dump in soap, and turn the dials on the washing machine (all of which kids love to do!), they have washed their own clothes, folded them, and put them in their drawers.

(A brief postscript—and praise. Today housework is no problem for either of my daughters. They've done it for years. They've developed the necessary skills. In fact, at one time the newlywed Courtney even earned extra money as her Proverbs 31 contribution to the income by cleaning the homes of others.)

Even if you share a room or an apartment, you still have your "house," your part of the place, to build. I talked with one ingenious mother of four little girls who share one bedroom. Each girl had her own bunk, shelves, and drawers to take care of. LaTonya also used masking tape to divide the floor space into four squares, making each daughter responsible for one square of the play area.

As I regularly reminded my daughters—and myself—"What you are at home is what you are!" We are either about the business of building the home, its atmosphere and its order, or we are pulling it down through destructive attitudes and neglect. How we take care of the place, the people, the checkbook(!), the clothes, etc., is very telling. Wisdom builds. Are we building?

Decide to begin building—It's never too late to begin—or begin again—to build your house, to create an enchanted oasis called "home." Only our enemy Satan would want us to think otherwise. We can begin at any time— even today.

> *Make a positive decision to do your work in the home willingly.*

A student in my "Woman After God's Own Heart" class wrote on her homework paper, "As I heard God's Word—and read it for myself in my Bible—I was so convicted I wanted to start right away to build my home. Putting God's principles to work in my home made an instant difference, so much so that my husband said last night, 'Gee, Kate, I'm glad you went to hear Elizabeth George!'" (I could only grin and give praise to God for what I had learned!)

Begin by making a positive decision (or by recommitting yourself) to do your work in the home "willingly" (Proverbs 31:13) and "heartily" (Colossians 3:23). The attitude of your heart is key. And don't forget to make another decision. Decide to immediately stop any destructive habits that are pulling down and destroying the little bit of heaven you are trying to build for others…and to the glory of God.

Each day, do one thing to build your home—I began to "each day do one thing to build my home" after reading an article I clipped out of the *Los Angeles Times* entitled "10 Good Reasons to Make the Bed." I confess I was a remedial case, and—you guessed it—I started making the bed each day because Reason #1 said, "Since the bed is the biggest item in the room, making the bed renders the whole room 80% better."[10]

Look around your home (or apartment or room or half a room), inside and out. Make a list of the things that need to be added, repaired, set up, etc., so that your area is more of a refuge. Then do just one item on your list each day—or even one each week.

You may also want to deal with one attitude that—if improved, if transformed by God—would enhance the atmosphere of the home. I used my own prayer notebook, for instance, to go to work on my nagging. After reading that it takes 21 days to eliminate a bad habit and form a new one, I thought, "Hey, I could do that with nagging!" Well, let me quickly tell you that it has taken much longer (decades longer!) than three weeks to lick this major problem area. But let me also tell you that every day and every effort does make a positive difference in my home, my family's heaven on earth.

Heart Response

In this single verse God gives us wisdom for a lifetime—"The wise woman builds her house, but the foolish pulls it down with her hands" (Proverbs 14:1). Search your heart and your home. As you consider these two women, which one is most like you? Where are you placing your focus and investing your energy? Look beneath the cleaning and cooking...to your heart.

Again, this book is all about taking God's wisdom and ways to heart, and I know you want what He wants. Respond to Him now by affirming that "the word of the Lord is right...the counsel of the Lord stands forever, the plans of His heart to all generations" (Psalm 33:4,11). God—who made us and knows us best—wants us to make a house a home, and He will help us do that.

14

A Heart That Watches Over the Home

She watches over the ways of her household.
PROVERBS 31:27

One of my most appalling memories from the days before I became a Christian is neglecting my household as, hour after hour, I sat curled up on our couch reading—and reading—and reading—anything and everything. Reading was a passion for me, something of far greater importance to me than a mere hobby or interest. And as I read, little Katherine and Courtney—wearing only diapers—roamed around the house unsupervised and untrained.

But thankfully, the minute Christ came into our home, He began to do His transforming work! I started attending a Bible study for young married women at my church on Wednesday nights. There, the powerful truth of God's Word turned my marriage upside down. (I should say right side up!). And there I studied *The Happy Home Handbook*,[1] which would turn my heart and home around.

Once I was in the Bible study, I used the corner of my couch for doing my weekly lesson (instead of reading for hours on end). One lesson had the (at least for me) utterly strange title "Why Work?" There I sat—my house ignored, my husband and children neglected—sifting through my new Bible to look up the Scripture references about work and why God thought work was so important. Soon I grabbed my pink marker to highlight another guideline God has given me as one of His homemakers.

Watching and Working

That guideline was tucked into that eye-opening description of the Proverbs 31 woman. The verse simply said, "She watches over the ways of her household, and does not eat the bread of idleness" (verse 27). Reading these 16 words, I suddenly knew that my couch days were over, but I performed one last act there. I reached for several of Jim's Bible reference books to find out what this "watching" meant.

I learned that as it is used here, "to watch" means "to hedge about" as with thorns, much like a mother bird or animal might do to protect her young. The verb expresses the active guarding, protecting, saving, and attending to something precious. This kind of watching involves observation and preservation. A woman who watches over the ways of her household is a woman who watches over her precious home.[2] Here was another aspect of my God-given goal, and I realized *I am on assignment from God to watch over my home and the people in it.*

To better understand the significance of the word *watch,* consider its use in Psalm 5:3—"My voice You shall hear in the morning, O Lord; in the morning I will direct it to You, and I will look up." "To look up" is the same Hebrew word as *watch.* The psalmist carefully prays to God in the morning and then becomes a lookout, keeping watch, being on the lookout, expecting his prayer to be answered.[3]

And there's more! *Watch* is used throughout the Bible to describe people who were posted to report the first sign of God's answers to prayer.[4] At the top of Mount Carmel, for instance, the prophet Elijah threw himself on the ground and began to pray. No rain had fallen for three-and-a-half years, and he began to beseech God for rain. As Elijah prayed, he had his servant run and look at the horizon for rain clouds, a sign that God was answering his prayer. Elijah prayed for rain seven times, and the servant looked out for the rain seven times—until there was an answer from God (1 Kings 18:41-44).

When you and I pray and as we watch over our homes, we must do so with the fervency and earnestness of an Elijah. This prophet and others like him spent their lives waiting, watching for God to fulfill the promises they'd spoken on His behalf. We are to be just as fervent as we make our houses homes and care for the people in them. Then we will be able to see and celebrate when God does His part—the answering, the blessing, the changing!

Looking Over the Functions of the Home

So what are some of the specific things you and I are to watch over in our homes? Maybe your list is like mine. In my home, I am the one who watches over safety, health, cleanliness, and security. (Whenever I'm gone, I leave instructions on the refrigerator door reminding Jim—and Katherine and Courtney, too, when they were older and living at home—to lock the doors at night because that's my job when I'm home.) And then there is the money—recording, saving, supervising, giving, spending, and stretching it.

> *What a great way to be a helper for your husband as you antici- pate, perceive, and act on needs in the home. Before your husband even thinks of some- thing, you have taken care of it!*

I also take care of clothing needs and maintenance, the appliance warranties and service contracts, and the food planning and preparation. As the one who does the grocery shopping and stocks the pantry and refrigera- tor, I watch over the nutrition, the selection, and the types of foods and beverages available in the house. I also oversee the calendar, keeping an eye open to upcoming events and trying to anticipate future needs. And all the while I intently watch over the attitudes and unexpressed needs of each family member.

Eighteenth-century preacher Jonathan Edwards was blessed to have a wife who watched over his home. He trusted every- thing to Sarah's care with complete confidence, and one partic- ular example shows what a true watcher is. One day Jonathan Edwards looked up from his stacks of books and studies and asked Sarah, "Isn't it about time for the hay to be cut?" Because she was a watcher and a worker, because she stood guard over what was precious, she was able to reply, "It's been in the barn for two weeks."[5]

What a blessing you can be to your family as you watch, as you keep a lookout over the various functions of the home. And what a great way to be a helper for your husband as you antici- pate, perceive, and act on needs in the home. Before your husband even *thinks* of something, you have taken care of it!

Yes, But How?

How can we place ourselves before God so He can grow in us

hearts that effectively watch over our precious homes? Here are some steps you can take as God cultivates such a heart in you.

Step 1: Understand that this role as helper and guard is God's plan for you—As Proverbs 31:10-31 illustrates, a woman after God's own heart—married or not—watches over the ways of her household and refuses to eat the bread of idleness (Proverbs 31:27). When I realized that these instructions were from God—and not from my mother or my husband or the woman teaching my class—I was hit hard by the truth, which is what I needed. And as I thought about all that is involved in first building the home and then watching over a household, I was shocked at the huge responsibility God has given me at home.

Furthermore, God calls me (and you) to be a "virtuous" woman (Proverbs 31:10), adding yet another challenge to our role in the home. The word *virtuous* means moral strength, strength of character. But a second meaning emphasizes physical ability and physical prowess. And Proverbs 31 is all about a virtuous woman in both senses of the word. This portrait reveals her strength of character and moral excellence as well as her strength of body—her industriousness, energy, work, skill, and accomplishments—as she watched over her precious household and refused to eat the bread of idleness.

As I looked at this excellent woman in all her splendor, I realized I had played up the moral aspect of virtue and downplayed the work part. Yet doing the work of watching is part of God's perfect plan for me—and you—as He grows us into women of excellence. Once we understand that, we are pointed in the right direction.

Step 2: Begin watching over your home (versus eating the bread of idleness)—When I learned about "watching," I realized that, at best, I was *glancing* over my house. My efforts were certainly nothing like what God describes in Proverbs 31. So I made some real—and difficult—decisions about watching (the positive) and about not eating the bread of idleness (the negative).

In a moment, I'll share some helpful time-management principles, but now I'll tell you about the *one* that governs all of my waking hours, all of my life—"In all labor there is profit" (Proverbs 14:23). This bit of wisdom has helped me become more of a watcher and less of an idler. Here's how I put it to work.

> *God's Word has worked for me, helping me tune my heart to His will and His ways. God is faithful and will do the same for you.*

Throughout the day, I tell myself, "Elizabeth, there is profit in all labor. It's great to keep the work in nice, neat piles labeled A-tasks, B-tasks, and C-tasks, but if you just keep moving, it'll all get done." So I keep moving all day long. I have lists and a general schedule (which can even include a break or a nap), but other than my quiet time (remember, our pursuit of God must come first), I'm busy doing something all day long.

Even when Katherine and Courtney were young, I set about to ingrain this principle in them so they wouldn't have the same struggles I had. So, for instance, they didn't watch TV unless they were doing something. That means that if they were watching TV, they were also busy organizing their school notebooks, covering books, cleaning out drawers, baking chocolate chip cookies, painting fingernails. On and on their TV activities went because there is profit in all labor.

While they were doing their busywork in front of the TV, so was I. I would go through my recipes, plan the menus for the upcoming week, read articles and clip coupons out of the newspaper, scan magazine articles, and sometimes paint my fingernails too.

One result of this training in busyness is that, to this day, none of us derives much pleasure from TV. We can all take it or leave it. We're unable to simply plop down and become engrossed in a television program. Put differently, we don't know how to eat the bread of idleness. To us, it tastes bad. And we do know how to get a lot of work done.

As this example shows, God's principles were His solutions to my disorganization and inefficiency in my home. I had to do a complete 180-degree turn. But I'm on the way (and so are my daughters as they watch over their homes and are now training their seven little ones), thanks to the instructions one woman after God's own heart found in the Bible. God's Word has worked for me, helping me tune my heart to His will and His ways. God is faithful and will do the same for you.

Step 3: Eliminate idleness—I'm not sure where Jim picked up the following list of "time robbers," but he passed it on to me, and I want to pass it on to you. Use it first to help you identify time robbers in your daily life and then to help you buy back time for watching and working in your precious home. Here are the major time robbers:

- Procrastination
- Inadequate personal planning and scheduling
- Interruptions by people without appointments (This includes interruptions by way of the telephone. And please note, your children are *not* interruptions—they are your greatest work and the best investment of your time!)

- Failure to delegate
- Poor use of the telephone
- Reading junk mail
- Lack of concern for good time management
- Unclear priorities

Which robber will you corral this week as you become a more alert, better watcher over your home?

Heart Response

Oh, my dear sister and friend, we must pray for eyes to see the vision God has for our precious home and for hearts to understand how important what happens in our home is to Him. May our goal be that our houses be made into homes that show forth God's desires for the beauty and purpose of those structures.

Do you see God's ideal for your home life? Do you see the value of every meal prepared, every rug vacuumed, every piece of furniture dusted, every floor mopped, every load of laundry washed, folded, and ironed? Is it your heart's desire to pay the price of watching and working?

Take inventory of your own heart attitude toward that precious place you call home. Are you praying—and then watching for the glory of God's answers? My friend Ginger recently started praying for her home. Hear what she reports:

> Every morning when I have my quiet time I go through the whole house and pray for each room. For the kitchen I pray that everything made there will show my love for my family. (All my recipes have long since been revised so

the fruit of the Spirit is added in—a pinch of love, a hand-
ful of patience, etc.) I pray that each room will be filled with
God's love and protection. This way I have a new outlook
on housework. It is no longer work. I am even able to sing
while I clean the bathroom!

Ask God to perform open-heart surgery in you. Ask Him to open it
up and fill it with His desires for your home and the strength and passion
to fulfill those desires.

15

A Heart That Creates Order from Chaos

I will therefore that the younger women...
guide the house.
1 TIMOTHY 5:14 (KJV)

I had heard about time management and organization but never paid much attention. Standing in the supermarket checkout line, I'd invariably see some magazine promising that an article inside would end my time-management problems once and for all. And, as a voracious reader, I spent a lot of time in bookstores, and there I would find whole rows of books on time management and organization. But for a long time I had zero motivation in this area.

Responsibility and Accountability

What finally did motivate me wasn't a magazine article or a book or a teacher or even my husband's pleas. It was God's Word! Continuing to read through my Bible using my pink marker to highlight those verses with special meaning to me as a woman, I found a verse that worked its way into my unorganized heart. There was no way I could miss the word "guide" as I read, "I will therefore that the younger women...guide the house" (1 Timothy 5:14 KJV). Other versions of the Bible read "preside over a home or be mistress of the house."[1] Either way, the message was clear.

Furthermore, the why of this statement was clear. Here's the situation Timothy faced: The young widows of Timothy's church were "idle, wandering about from house to house, and not only idle but also gossips and busybodies, saying things which they ought not" (1 Timothy 5:13). Their loose, undisciplined behavior led those outside the church to think and speak poorly of Christianity (verse 14). Obviously, having a home to manage would contribute positively to these women's lives by, at the very least, eliminating the opportunity for these negative behaviors.

God was speaking to me! I was certainly idle and guilty of a few of the other bad behaviors mentioned in this passage. Clearly I needed to take action and make some changes. But first, to be sure I was headed in the right direction, I wanted to get a handle on the meaning of *guide*.

> *Every day we are called to manage what God has given us, what He has provided through our husbands' efforts and our own.*

To "guide a house" means to be the head of or to rule a family, to guide the home. The one who manages a house is the goodman of the house, the householder.[2] Yet this management has built-in accountability, describing as it does the work of a steward or a servant. The woman who manages her house is *not* the head of the home (her husband is if she is married, and God is if she is not). Instead, she is the householder, the home manager.

Many of Jesus' parables offer us insight into this kind of management. In these stories that teach a lesson about God's kingdom, Jesus generally describes a landowner who, taking a leave of absence, delegates the work and the goods of the house to his householder and manager. The most familiar of these is the parable of the talents (see Matthew 25:14-30). When the owner returned from a long journey, he called all his servants together so they could give an account of the work they did while he was gone.

Whether we realize it or not, this parable reflects what you and I do in the home. Every day we are called to manage what God has given us, what He has provided through our husbands' efforts and our own. What a blessing it is to us when we serve Him well in this capacity. And what a blessing we are to our family when we properly manage the house. In fact, Martin Luther wrote, "The greatest blessing…is to have a wife to whom you may entrust your affairs."[3] That's what being a home manager is all about!

Yes, But How?

How does a woman who wants what God wants, a woman who wants to know order instead of chaos, a woman after God's own heart, manage her home? Let me tell you how I began to manage our home.

First, understand that home management is God's best for us— God isn't asking His women to *like* being a home manager (although that comes with time as we reap the multitude of blessings that result from better home management). And God isn't asking us to *feel like* managing our home. He is simply calling us to do it. Home management is His plan, His way. It's His good and acceptable and perfect will for us (Romans 12:2). It's His "best" for us. Remember the saying that helps me make decisions? "Good, better, best, never let it rest, until your good is better and your better best." Choosing to manage our homes is choosing God's best for us.

Second, decide to take home management seriously—Why? Because God uses the management of the home as a training ground for our usefulness in the church. How well you and I maintain our personal relationship with God, how devotedly we love our husbands and our children, and how effectively we manage the home indicates how well we would manage a ministry. It's true that what we are at home is what we are!

> *If we manage our homes effectively, we will have time to be involved in church ministry.*

If, for instance, I do a poor job at home, I'll do a poor job in the church. If I take shortcuts at home, I'll do the same in ministry. If I'm a sloppy manager at home, I'll be a sloppy manager at church. Such poor habits become a lifestyle.

But the opposite is also true. If I am organized in the home, I'll probably be organized in my church ministries. If I am a good steward of the responsibilities of the home, I'll probably be a good steward of the responsibilities of ministry outside the home. Jesus said, "He who is faithful in what is least is faithful also in much; and he who is unjust in what is least is unjust also in much" (Luke 16:10).

I realized that—as much as I wanted to—I couldn't run out the front door of my home, leaving it in a shambles, and go over to the church to do the work of ministry. I came to understand that God has charged me with the stewardship of managing my home, and He uses this primary area of ministry to train me for managing other areas of ministry. At home, as I try to live according to God's instructions to me, instructions I find in His written Word, I develop faithfulness and learn to follow through. At home I became a faithful steward (1 Corinthians 4:2), which prepared me for other areas of faithful stewardship.

Once I have shown myself to be a faithful manager at home, I am more free to run out the door and do the work of ministry outside my home. And the same applies to going to a job. All is well at home. Everything is somewhat under control. The people are cared for, and the place is cared for. My management responsibilities on the domestic front are fulfilled.

And let me be clear: I'm not talking about years and decades spent at home waiting for the children to grow up and leave so we have less at home to manage. That option wouldn't teach our children much about the importance of being a contributing member of the body of Christ, the church. But if we manage our homes effectively (and you'll find more about this in the final section of this book), we will have time to be involved in church ministry in some capacity.

On a daily basis, management of the home happens—and happened—for me when I have a schedule. At certain times I plan to do housework. I always reserve time for cultivating my relationship with Jim and, in the past (and to a great extent even today although they live thousands of miles away), with Katherine and Courtney. Although I was not able to be involved in all the ministries I'd like to, I was always involved in *something* at church. The point is, order emerges out of chaos when we schedule what's important.

Third, live as though you will be accountable for the condition of your home and the use of your time...because you will!—In fact, when our husbands (or anyone else) walk in the door and look around the house, we have just revealed what we've been doing in response to God's call to us to manage the home. What do people see when they enter your house? Do they find calm—or chaos? Peace—or panic? Palace—or pigpen? Evidence of preparation—or procrastination?

Now think for a moment about the feeling you get when you enter a hotel room. What greets you? Order. Quiet. Cleanliness. You can still see the vacuum tracks in the carpet. The bed is made (and remember it occupies 80 percent of the visual space in a room!). The last sheet of toilet paper has been folded to a point. No TV or stereo blares. Order reigns. Someone has done the work of effective management, and his or her efforts make the room a sanctuary.

> *How would the Lord—and your family—rate your service, your meals, and your management?*

I well remember the day Jim and I checked out of just such a place. We had been staying in a hotel for six days while Jim was processed at the Army Headquarters in Los Alamitos, California, for five months of active duty. Although Jim was in the ministry, he had been a pharmacy officer in the U.S. Army Reserves since college. This was our first time for activation and deployment in over 30 years... and off he went via military aircraft to Fort Benning, Georgia, and then on to Wuerzburg, Germany, for five months.

Anyway, Los Alamitos was too far from our home for Jim to commute back and forth for the six days. Hence, the hotel stay. And the entire time we were there, I had that feeling of order despite the fact it was a time of great chaos for our family.

When we checked out of the hotel, the hotel clerk gave me a

card to fill out, rating the facilities and the service we had received during our stay. It was a pleasure to give a top rating on every count. We had been well taken care of. The hotel staff met our needs as they took care of our room and our food, even giving me a 30 percent discount on meals!

As I filled out that evaluation card, I wondered how the Lord—and my family—would rate my service, my meals, and my management. With the Lord's grace and with management skills I've learned and practiced over the years, I'm doing better every day. God's ways work!

Twelve Tips for Time Management

When Jim was a seminary student, I went with him to the campus every Friday and spent the entire day in the library. I found the time-management section and systematically read each book in it, jotting down principles from all of them. So now, as we consider time management and organization in the home, I want to share with you my top 12 time-management principles, the ones that made the greatest difference in my home by helping me know order in chaos.

1. *Plan in detail*—Have a planner and write everything down in it. I've found that the more you plan, the better you manage and the more you achieve. Also, the more detailed your plans are, the better. Try planning twice a day—last thing in the evening and first thing in the morning. (More about this in chapter 22!)

2. *Deal with today*—All God asks of you and me is to handle and manage today, only today. Jesus said, "Do not worry about tomorrow, for tomorrow will worry about its own things. Sufficient for the day is its own trouble" (Matthew 6:34). God also says,

"*This* is the day the Lord has made; we will rejoice and be glad in *it*" (Psalm 118:24). Saint Augustine paraphrased Psalm 90:12, "Number every day as your last day."

Each day is important in and of itself:

- What you are today is what you are becoming.
- You are today what you have been becoming.
- Every day is a little life, and our whole life is but a day repeated.

3. *Value each minute*—Know how long it will take you to complete each task in your home. Are you facing a 2-minute task or a 20-minute one? Then decide if the task is the best use of the time. And how much is a minute worth? It's priceless or worthless—depending on how you use it.

4. *Keep moving*—Remember the principle of momentum: "A body at rest [human or otherwise] tends to remain at rest, and a body in motion tends to remain in motion." Use this law of physics to your advantage. Tell yourself, "Just one more thing…just five more minutes." Keep moving and you can cross one more thing off your "to do" list!

5. *Develop a routine*—Or, as the experts say, try "horizontal" planning. "Trying to do the same thing at the same time each day conserves and generates energy. It conserves energy by cutting down on indecision. You perform menial tasks by rote. It generates energy through habit—the habit of expecting to make phone calls, plan the meals, read the paper, attend a class, or go to a meeting—at a particular time."[4] Try to put as many tasks as possible into a routine.

6. *Exercise and diet*—Studies show that exercise increases

metabolism, creates energy, causes you to sleep better, and produces pleasure hormones that contribute to positive attitudes, joy in life, and a general lust for life. Also, don't be spooked by the word "diet." The word simply means "a way of life." So develop a dietary "way of life" that gives you the energy and health you need to accomplish God's best.

7. *Ask the "half the time" question*—"If my life depended upon doing this task in half the time I have allotted, what shortcuts would I take?" Then take them.

8. *Use a timer for everything*—Whatever the task, use your timer. (I'm using one right this minute, and its ticking is pushing me forward.) Setting the timer for "just five minutes" can get you started. Setting the timer for "I'll quit in five minutes" can keep you going. Also, when you set the timer, try to beat the clock. After all, as Parkinson's Law says, "Work expands to fill the time allowed for its completion." The timer helps you allow less time. And there's something extremely motivating about hearing your life tick away!

9. *Do the worst first*—What is the worst task on your to-do list? Do it first and you'll keep that heavy cloud of dread from hanging over you all day long. Use your timer to help you get started. And once that worst is done, your attitude will be greatly improved, and you'll have more energy for the tasks that remain.

10. *Read daily on time management*—Just five minutes a day will help motivate you. If you don't have a good time-management book, start by reading over these 12 principles every day.

11. *Say no*—Make your schedule. Let it be Plan A. Then

follow your plan by saying no to yourself and to others. Move to Plan B only if God is moving you to Plan B.

12. *Begin the night before*—Look what you can do the night before!

> Plan the next day
> Plan the next day's meals
> Select, lay out, and prepare clothes
> Clean up the kitchen
> Run the dishwasher
> Set the table for the next meal
> Tidy up the house
> Prepare lunches and meals
> Defrost meat
> Sort the wash and get a load going in the
>   washer
> Put things you need to take with you by the
>   door

Little steps like these can bring great results when it comes to time management and being organized at home. I've also noticed that these little steps snowball. Once you get started, you'll find energy and enthusiasm to keep moving.

Heart Response

Before we leave the subject of order in the home, let's take a look at the heart of the home—which is your heart! What is your attitude toward your home and your housework? Is your heart in tune with God's? Are you desiring what He desires for the management and guidance of your home? Do you want to be the home manager God wants you to be? Do you acknowledge that responsibilities at home grow greater character... that managing your home enhances the lives of those you live with...and that a well-organized home makes for far better service to the Lord and His people? Ask God to help you move toward better management—and don't wory: Slowly but surely counts.

16

A Heart That Weaves a Tapestry of Beauty

Admonish the young women…
to be homemakers.
TITUS 2:4-5

As God's women, you and I are blessed with the God-given assignment to weave a tapestry of beauty in our homes. One devotional writer of old saw the noble role as "making home first of all a center of attraction by its order and cleanliness and comfort; then by its harmonies of peace and love, so that no discordant notes may mar the music of its joy; and then by…securing the safety of economy and the honor of a wife who 'weaves' all into beauty and order at home."[1]

This is exactly what a woman after God's own heart would gladly spend her life trying to achieve! But, as always, we must first adapt His *attitude* in our hearts if we are to *act* in ways that glorify Him.

Beauty from Busyness

As I continued searching God's Word, He whet my appetite for His kind of home and the beauty that comes when we serve Him there. I found a gold mine—and used my pink marker a lot—in the small book of Titus. In Titus 2:3-5 I found yet another vision for my efforts at home in these words: "Admonish the young women to be...home-makers" (verse 5).

> *To successfully make the home of my dreams and God's call a reality, I have to be there, working and weaving on it every day.*

I don't know about you, but I had an aversion to that word *homemakers*—until I discovered what God had in mind. Before that, it sounded like dull labor and mundane chores. But looking once again at Jim's study books, I learned that to be a homemaker means to be a stayer-at-home, to be domestically inclined, a good housekeeper, and a keeper at home.[2] Another source emphasized that a woman's primary sphere of activity and contribution is the home,[3] and still another concluded that we are to be active in or busy with household duties.[4] The commentary that most moved my heart said that I am simply to be a "home lover."[5]

Any woman who carries in her mind and heart the thought "Home sweet home!" qualifies as a home lover. That term definitely portrays a fitting *attitude* in response to the call of Titus 2:4-5, but weaving a tapestry of beauty in our homes also calls for *action*. To successfully make the home of my dreams and God's call a reality, I have to be there, working and weaving on it every day. I have to plan the picture and select the colors, threads, and textures. I have to know what I want the finished tapestry to look like. And I have to pay attention to details along the way.

This project called "home" takes effort and time each day.

The effort and the activity—the time, the work, the care, and the mental and physical muscle—combine to make a home beautiful. Such beauty comes when I am active at home, busy responding to the call and challenge and joy of weaving a tapestry there.

Yes, But How?

How does a woman who wholeheartedly wants to weave a tapestry of beauty in her home begin?

Understand the beauty and blessings of God's will for you—God is teaching us His will when He calls us to be homemakers. And I figure that if God calls me to serve at home, to be on top of things, and to see that my good housekeeping chores get done, then I want to do just that. So I resolved (and you may want to do the same) to be at home more often.

Now, *by faith,* I stay at home more often than I might naturally choose, keeping and caring for and loving my home, trusting God to bless my obedience. Oh, I'm not home all the time, but I am there much more than I was. And there are many blessings. For starters, when I'm home, I'm spending less money… because I'm not shopping. I'm also eating fewer calories because somehow, when I'm out, I usually end up eating out. And I'm saving the time and gas money it takes to go somewhere in the car. The ultimate bonus, though—and God knew this would be the case—has been the sense of well being I've experienced. I can see that all is well at home, that everything is under control (at least generally anyway!). The priceless reality of well being has come simply because I have chosen to spend a little more time at home.

Hear what happened when one dear woman in my "Women

After God's Own Heart" class made that same choice. She wrote:

> In the past, each new day would present many choices of who I would visit, where I would go, or what I would do! When my husband came home, he'd be lucky to find the bed made, much less something even defrosted for dinner. I really did not enjoy being home, as I am a people person and even put friends above my family.
>
> I am very happy to say that God has completely turned my life and priorities around as a result of my discovering *His* plan for my days. I now roll out of bed and make the bed immediately, and I'm learning to establish chores to do each day to keep my house in order. I plan my menus two weeks in advance and now have dinner cooking before my husband comes in the door.
>
> What a joy it has become to choose my husband, children, and home before other things, and it brings *real* satisfaction and contentment I've never known before.

Isn't this a beautiful picture—and a beautiful tapestry?

Understand that homemaking can be learned—Sadly, effective housekeeping isn't one of the many spiritual blessings we receive immediately and automatically when we become Christians. (Eternal life, the Holy Spirit dwelling within us, forgiveness for our sin, to name a few, are.) But the how-to's of homemaking can be learned, and Scripture says in Titus 2:3-5 that older women in the faith are to assist and teach younger women these how-to's.

This concept gave me so much hope, because—as I've tried to tell you—I was certainly clueless about making our house a home. So I began to look around for one of these Titus 2-type older women, someone who had her act together at home. Well, thank the Lord, I didn't have to look very far—her husband was our Sunday school teacher!

Meet Jane! Jane is an amazing woman, clearly a woman after God's own heart. Although we were the same age, she seemed to possess the wisdom of a woman a quarter of a century older than me. As I watched her, I saw character that spoke of her carefully nurtured relationship with God. When I saw Jane with her husband, I saw a woman who helped, followed, respected, and loved her husband. And her two preschool-age boys were obedient, polite, and definitely under control.

Well, Jim helped me find the courage to call Jane and ask to meet with her. She was absolutely delighted (I could hear it in her voice). And do you know where she wanted to meet? In her home where—like its mistress—everything was clean, neat, efficient, tidy, and in order. (Notice that I didn't say "a large, gorgeous showplace.")

I praise the Lord that Jane spent that time with me because she gave me the initial direction and nudge for me to tackle weaving my own tapestry. We first talked at length about her devotional life. Besides telling me exactly what she studied and how she did it, she showed me where she studied and let me peek at her prayer book.

Then we talked about marriage. She suggested a list of books to read and, again, shared with me *exactly* how she tried to love and serve her husband. The same with her sons. Jane made me privy to her personal and biblical principles for discipline, training, instruction, and love in the home.

Finally we got to the matter of the home itself, and I really got a bonus. Jane took me on a tour of her little house, opening cupboards, drawers, closets, and doors. I was speechless: The insides of her house didn't look like the insides of mine. And don't get me wrong. Jane wasn't bragging or boasting. She was *teaching* (that's what the Bible says older women are to do for younger ones). She was showing me a system that worked for her. She showed me how she kept her home neat in a minimum of time.

I can still hear Jane instructing me in her kitchen. She stooped down to the lower cabinet cupboards and opened the doors. There were the dishes. She explained, "My principle is 'a place for everything and everything in its place.' And right here is the place for the dishes and napkins. It's right next to the dishwasher so when my sons unload the dishwasher they can put them right here on their own level. Then, when it's time for them to set the table, they can easily get to the dishes and napkins."

You can't put a price on a lesson like that! I got it all, I heard it all, and I *saw* it all. Those few hours with Jane were definitely life changing!

Meet Beverly! I had another friend who taught me how to clean my house. It all began with a ministry call. I was organizing a planning meeting for our women's committee at church, and Beverly said, "Don't plan it for Friday because that's the day I clean my house!" She sounded so excited about her housekeeping plans that I asked if I could come over some Friday and watch her clean.

She said "Sure!" So we set a date and I went to Beverly's house...on a Friday morning. Well, while I was there I got another invaluable lesson. Beverly started on the worst first—her bathrooms. I saw exactly how she cleaned them, the products she used to clean them with, and her assortment of brushes, scrub sponges, scrapers, and cloths. Then she showed me how she cleaned each room—in a circle, starting just to the left of the door and moving item by item around the room. She was done in minutes!

I also remember reading about discipleship groups in another book by Anne Ortlund, which met (guess where?) in her home. At the first meeting, Anne shared, she takes the group through her home and tells them, "Well, this is my house. This is me. You are welcome to look in any drawer or cupboard or room or closet or book. What you find there will be me. The real me."[6]

Be home more often—My dear husband Jim unknowingly made a major contribution to the beauty of our home. As a young mom with two little ones and a home to maintain, I began to whine and complain to Jim, "I don't know what's wrong—I just can't seem to get anything done." Well, Jim—an expert on time management and a man with the spiritual gift of administration—was the wrong person to sound off to.

First he told me to get my calendar (a novel idea!). Then, once I had it spread out on the kitchen table, he said, "Now, Liz, which day do you need to do something out of the house?" Well, of course I said Wednesday. That's the day of our women's Bible study at church, and I definitely wanted—and desperately needed—to be there.

Then Jim stated, "OK, Wednesday is your day out. I want you to try to do all your errands and running around and

> *I am so thankful that my wise Jim helped me structure my life so I could be busy at home, using my time and energy to weave something beautiful, something of eternal value.*

visiting with friends on Wednesday, and be at home the rest of the week."

Although he didn't actually say it, I was grounded. But oh, how many times since then have I thanked Jim—and God—for that guidance. His simple piece of advice changed my life and helped turn our home into a tapestry of beauty. To this day, and throughout the decades, whether my house was full of kids or an empty nest, I still aim at leaving the house for errands or visiting or ministry purposes no more than once during the week.

Only later did I find a proverb that spoke of the value of Jim's advice—"Wisdom is in the sight of him who has understanding, but the eyes of a fool are on the ends of the earth" (Proverbs 17:24). In other words, wisdom sees the thing straight in front of us, the thing between our own two feet—and that is our home. The wise woman realizes the value of being home. But the foolish woman (which is what I was) is always looking "out there" (in the mall, in the outlet stores, in a friend's home, etc.) for fulfillment, excitement, activity, and meaning. I am so thankful that my wise Jim helped me structure my life so I could be busy at home, using my time and energy to weave something beautiful, something of eternal value. Even today, I still follow this weekly plan of one day out because it worked so well for me.

I want to quickly say that I too have known a variety of lifestyles. I've been a full-time executive secretary, a full-time teacher, a night-school teacher, a stay-at-home mom, a part-time teacher, and a part-time bookkeeper in my home.

Now I work full-time-plus helping manage all that is involved in our expanding multigenerational family and the ministry my husband and I enjoy...plus Jim and I travel regularly to speak... and we both try to write every day. My days begin early and last long into the night because I have not only my "work" to do, but am still hard at work letting God use me to weave His beauty into the tapestry of our home. You see, whatever my "work" is, my husband, children, grandchildren, and home will always be a higher priority and more important to me. My work, my ministry, is further down the list of God's priorities for me. (More on this later.) Near the top, right behind the *people* in my life—my husband, my children, and my grandchildren—is taking care of the *place* of home, being a home lover, a homemaker.

After all, no one is responsible for managing the George home (the people as well as the place) except me. So I've said no to many things I really like to do so that I can have the time at home to keep working on my tapestry of beauty. For instance, I rarely go out to lunch. I shop by mail or online, if at all. I've given up long, extended visits on the phone. I've even had to whittle my reading down to what is essential. All these changes (and others) came when I decided to spend more time at home and on my home.

I told you I was a voracious reader, and one clever book on home management contained a chapter title that caused me to chuckle—"This Little Piggy Stayed Home!" Doesn't that say it all? I watched the two authors of this book, the "side-tracked sisters," interviewed on NBC's *The Today Show* about the principles in their best-selling book. The main principle is "Never leave the house before you've done all the…duties for the day." There's no way to keep from having an orderly home if you follow this advice. But it does require one thing—you'll have to spend some time at home to get the daily work done!

Organize your outings—It took me a while, but I soon realized that I couldn't, for instance, just run to the cleaners. Instead, I understood for the first time that I needed to stop by the cleaners when I was running all my other errands. I developed an "on the way" routine that covered all my errands—the carpool *and* the cleaners *and* the post office *and* the bank *and* the grocery store *and* any other necessary stops.

If you have a job outside the home, consider these two ways to be better organized so you can spend more time at home. First, run errands on the way to and from work. And second, use your lunch hour!

One morning while I was at the cleaners, I saw the ultimate example of this "on the way" practice. A Volkswagen bug pulled up (in the fire lane!) and the woman driving it jumped out of the car without even turning off the engine. She grabbed her dirty clothes, dashed in, and threw them on the counter while the clerk ran to get her cleaned ones. Out she ran (literally), off to the next stop on her list. Now picture this: She was wearing a business suit and her errand running shoes—her tennis shoes—and her hair was in hot rollers! It was 8:15 in the morning, and this woman was running her errands "on the way" to work.

Perhaps like that woman, I've read many insightful books specifically for working women. Their main piece of advice has to do with the use of discretionary time—time that is considered to belong to the employee to use any way she likes. Discretionary time includes the lunch hour. You see, a working woman can either spend her lunch hour visiting or gossiping and listening to empty talk and complaints, or she can spend it (as the books suggest) going to the post office, grocery shopping for nonperishables, making important phone calls, or doing a multitude of other things that make it possible for her to *go home* the second work is over.

If you have a job outside the home, consider these two ways to be better organized so you can spend more time at home. First, run errands on the way to and from work. And second, use your lunch hour. You'll be more content when you arrive home, and therefore more able to be the kind of homemaker you and God want you to be.

Heart Response

Now, dear fellow weaver, take God's teaching to heart. Do you cherish your home? Is it "home sweet home" to you? When you are away from it, do you yearn for it? Is your heart truly centered in your home? Are the place and the people there more important to you than anyone or anything else?

When I responded to God's call to homemaking and to questions like these so many years ago, I wrote out an "I will" list about my home sweet home. (Earlier I had gone through the book of Psalms, writing out every "I will" uttered by the psalmist, which I thought was a good exercise for doing business with God.) I called my covenant with God "The Heart of a Homemaker." You'll notice that it touches on much of what you've read so far.

1. I will get up before my family in order to prepare myself spiritually and physically.

2. I will prepare breakfast for my family and sit with them while they eat.

3. I will work diligently to send every member of my family off in a good mood.

4. I will consult my husband every day to see if there is anything special he wants me to do for him.

5. I will keep a neat and orderly home.

6. I will respond positively.

7. I will seek to meet my husband's needs.

8. I will put my husband before my children.

9. I will personally meet and greet each family member as he or she returns home.

10. I will be predictably happy.

11. I will prepare special, good food for my family.

12. I will make dinner a special time.

13. I will grow daily in the areas of the Lord, marriage, family, and homemaking.

Is yours the heart of a homemaker? For help, ask God for His transforming touch. As He empowers you to obey, He will give you joy at the task to which He calls you and enhance the beauty of the tapestry you are weaving.

17

A Heart Strengthened by Spiritual Growth

Grow in the grace and knowledge
of our Lord and Savior Jesus Christ.
2 PETER 3:18

As I'm sure you can tell, the book of Proverbs is a delight to me. I love God's refreshing wisdom, and I love the woman pictured at the end of the book, the Proverbs 31 woman (verses 10-31). Whenever I read those verses, this excellent woman reminds me of a watch. From the outside, we see her hands moving. We witness all the activity of those 22 verses, her busyness as she lives out her assignments from God as wife, mother, and homemaker. But

> *I have learned what keeps us fresh and excited and motivated in our godly pursuits—and this is spiritual growth.*

there's something inside, something deep within her heart, that makes her tick, moving her along, energizing her efforts, and motivating her activity.

You and I need that same God-given something inside to empower our actions as women after His heart. As we go about fulfilling God's assignment to us as women—whether we're married or not, whether we're moms or not—there has to be a *Mover* inside our heart or we won't become women after God's own heart. If there's nothing inside, without God's Spirit inside, we won't be able to keep on keeping on. We won't be able to find the strength to faithfully carry out God's Word and His will. We won't be able to finish the path we've started out on.

Well, I have learned what keeps us fresh and excited and motivated in our godly pursuits—and that is spiritual growth. Our spiritual growth in Jesus Christ—growing to be more like Him strengthens our hearts, fills them, and empowers us to obey His commands.

Spiritual Growth Begins in Jesus Christ

You and I have two options for how we live. We can live our lives with Jesus Christ or without Him. It's a clear-cut black/white, either/or situation. The Bible says, "This is the testimony: that God has given us eternal life, and this life is in His Son. He who has the Son has life; he who does not have the Son of God does not have life" (1 John 5:11-12). As this Scripture tells us, there is *no* life without Jesus Christ!

That's the frightening condition I lived in for 28 years. I grew up in a wonderful home with loving parents who were faithful to take me to church and expose me to God's truth both there and daily at home. But several key pieces were missing from my spiritual understanding. One of those pieces was accurate knowledge of who Jesus Christ is. I loved Him and believed that He was the Son of God, but it never clicked that being the *Son of God* meant He *was* God. Only by eventually reading a book filled with clear teaching from the Scriptures did I grow to understand that Jesus Christ was God in flesh, living on earth, and dying on a cross to save sinners like me and give us eternal life.

The second missing piece was a biblical understanding of sin. I'm still amazed when I think about all those years I truly loved God, loved Jesus, loved the Bible, believed in the Holy Spirit and the miracles of the Bible, and even prayed. I was a "good" person (I didn't steal or murder), and I thought that was all that mattered. I had no knowledge of the fact of personal sin—that "*all* have sinned and fall short of the glory of God" (Romans 3:23 NIV). And since I didn't sin—the logic went—I didn't need a savior!

I've told you a little about my early life—that Jim and I began our marriage without God, that I was venturing down a path that led me away from my husband and children. One day, standing in the middle of the kitchen with little Katherine hanging on one leg and littler Courtney on the other, I raised my fists to the ceiling and yelled, "There has *got* to be more to life than this!" Hearing this cry of desperation, God began to move me toward Him and a complete knowledge of Him, His Son, *and* my sin. When He was done with me, I realized at last that *I needed a Savior!* And what did I find in Jesus, my Savior?

A new beginning—When you and I come to a saving knowledge of Jesus Christ, we are given a new beginning, a fresh start, forgiveness for the past, wisdom for handling life, and power for doing what's right. The apostle Paul explains it like this: "If anyone is in Christ, he is a new creation; old things have passed away; behold, all things have become new" (2 Corinthians 5:17).

God's love and acceptance—Whenever I am down, discouraged, doubting, depressed, defeated, or dismayed (someone once quipped that all these "D" words are from the Devil!), I stop and remind myself, "No matter what has happened, no matter what life looks like, no matter what you're feeling, you are accepted in the Beloved—and nothing else matters!" Indeed, God has "made us *accepted* in the Beloved" (Ephesians 1:6)!

God's power in the Holy Spirit—Can you imagine having the power of God at work in your life? When Christ is your Savior, that's what happens. God empowers you through His Holy Spirit to do good, to effect change in your life, to make your life fulfilling and meaningful, to help others, and to minister for Christ. Jesus said, "You shall receive *power* when the Holy Spirit has come upon you" (Acts 1:8).

God's total sufficiency—No matter what the problem, the hurdle, the struggle, the suffering you face, God promises, "My grace is sufficient for you" (2 Corinthians 12:9). Whether you're dealing with temptation, a difficult marriage, problems with the children, needs in the home, personal challenges, loneliness, demands at work, health issues, a stretching ministry, or any other difficult situation, God promises, "My grace is sufficient for you."

Spiritual Growth Involves the Pursuit of Knowledge

In addition to being our Savior, Jesus is our model for how to live a life that pleases God. When we look at His life, we see that "Jesus increased in wisdom" (Luke 2:52). One proverb (a constant challenge to me) reflects the importance of such growth stating, "The heart of him who has understanding seeks knowledge, but the mouth of fools feeds on foolishness" (Proverbs 15:14). Put another way, an intelligent person purposefully seeks knowledge,

Phil 4:8 - whatever is true ▽

but fools nibble randomly, vacantly chewing on words and ideas that have no value, no flavor, and no nutrition.

What are you and I feeding our minds? Are we heeding this biblical warning about the danger of "garbage in, garbage out"? May we *purposefully* seek knowledge and guard against spending precious time on things that have no value. One way I guard my mind is by following the advice of a special woman, advice that has provided help for living a godward life as well as fodder for teaching, books, study materials, and ministry. She told me, "Elizabeth, you've got to have five fat files!" *Psalm 91:4*

John 8:32 - truth will set you free *His truth will be your shield*

Create five fat files—You're probably as puzzled as I was when I heard her say these words, so let me explain. But even before I do, take the first step and purchase or round up five manila file folders.

Aim at expertise—Next, select five areas you'd like to become an expert in and label a file for each of them. A word of caution: choose areas from the spiritual realm. Remember the proverb? You don't want to feed on pursuits that have no value. Instead choose topics of eternal value. To help you determine those five areas, answer the questions, "What do you want to be known for?" and "What topics do you want your name associated with?"

> *Personal spiritual growth is all about preparation for ministry. It's about filling yourself up first so that you have something to give.*

I have a friend, for instance, whose name many people associate with prayer. Whenever we needed someone at church to teach on prayer, lead a day of prayer for our women, or open a meeting with worship prayer, everyone automatically thinks of her. For more than 20 years, she has been studying what the Bible teaches about prayer, looking closely at the men and women of the Bible who prayed, reading about prayer, and praying. Prayer is definitely one of her areas of expertise, one of her five fat files. Another friend is known for her knowledge of the Bible. Whenever the women at church needed someone to lead a survey of the Bible or give an overview of the prophets, we would call on Betty. Still another friend speaks to church groups about time management. These three women have become experts.

Through the years, I've compiled a list of the fat files that the students in my "Woman After God's Own Heart" class kept. I now share some of the topics to stimulate your thinking. They range from the practical—hospitality, health, child-raising, home-making, Bible-study methods—to the theological—attributes of God, faith, fruit of the Spirit. They include areas for minis-try—biblical counseling, teaching, serving, women's ministry—as well as areas of character—the devotional life, heroes of the faith, love, virtues of godliness. They center around lifestyles—single-ness, parenting, organization, widowhood, the pastor's home—and zero in on the personal—holiness, self-control, submission, contentment. Wouldn't you love to sit in on the classes these women may teach in ten years—or read the books they may even-tually write? After all, such personal spiritual growth is all about preparation for ministry. It's about filling yourself up first so that you have something to give in ministry!

Fill the files—Now start putting information into your files. They'll get fat as you follow the exhortation to "read everything on [your] subject...articles, books, specialized magazines, and news clippings...attend seminars...teach on the subject(s)... spend time with those who are the best in these areas, picking their brains....seek and sharpen your expertise."[1]

Most importantly, read your Bible to see firsthand what God says about your areas of interest. After all, His thoughts are the primary knowledge you want. I even code my Bible. You know by now that pink highlights passages of interest to women, and you're probably not surprised to learn that one of my five fat files is "Women." Besides marking those passages in pink, I've put a "W" in the margin beside them. Anything in my Bible that relates to women, wives, mothers, homemakers, or women of the Bible has a "W" beside it. I did the same thing with "T" for teaching, "TM" for time management, etc. Once you pick your areas and set up your code, I guarantee you'll be so excited and motivated that you'll wake up *before* the alarm clock rings eager to open God's Word, pen in hand, to look for His wisdom about the areas where you want wisdom!

And as you continue your quest for knowledge about five spiritual topics, remember that you are working on this personal growth in order to minister to others. I made a fresh commitment regarding eternal matters because I was so sobered by Jim's mother's memorial service. As I told you earlier, Lois exemplified the saying,

> Only one life, 'twill soon be past,
> only what's done for Christ will last.

Each morning Lois filled her mind with the things of God, and then she spent the rest of that day allowing that fullness to fill others in ministry. We are saved to serve (2 Timothy 1:9), and serving requires that we be full of things eternal, things worth sharing. Our fullness becomes the overflow that is our ministry. It's what we have to give and pass on to others. As a dear mentor constantly drilled into me, "Nothing going in equals nothing going out!"

Spiritual Growth Includes Stewardship of Your Body *discipline and reaching goals*

You may have been hoping this subject wouldn't come up, but we're told in the Bible that how we manage our body affects our ministry and the quality of our lives. The apostle Paul put it this way: "I discipline my body and bring it into subjection, lest, when I have preached to others, I myself should become disqualified" (1 Corinthians 9:27).

The goal in the physical realm is discipline, the self-control that is a gift of God's grace (Galatians 5:23). His Spirit in us gives us strength to resist temptation, to control our appetite rather than allowing it to control us, and to train our body into obedience.

Every time I ask a woman who is enjoying an energetic life and ministry how she does it, I cringe a bit as she says the two predictable words—*diet* and *exercise*. If the goal is a quality of life filled with quality days of serving the Lord, attention to the body is key!

Spiritual Growth Means Becoming Like Jesus

As Jesus grew up, He increased not only in wisdom (the mind) and stature (the body), but He also increased in favor with God (Luke 2:52). Oh to be like Jesus! How can you and I grow in this direction?

Increase in knowledge—As we've seen, Jesus is our model. God desires for us to follow in His footsteps and grow in the knowledge

having a plan and goals in place - have a direction you are heading

of God (Colossians 1:10) as well as in the grace and knowledge of our Lord and Savior Jesus Christ (2 Peter 3:18). Like Paul's prayer for the church in Philippi, our prayer for ourselves should be that our "love may abound still more and more in knowledge and all discernment" (Philippians 1:9). And we should be doing something with all that knowledge, for we are to be *doers* of the word, not hearers only (James 1:22)!

Have a plan—Increasing in knowledge is a lot like getting the evening meal on the table. You have to have a plan. When it comes to making dinner, you know that you have to do certain things at certain times if your family is to sit down at a designated time in the evening and eat. Likewise, when it comes to increasing your knowledge of God, you have to do a certain thing (sit down) in a certain place (your place) with certain items (pen, paper, reading schedule, study guide, whatever you need) at a specific time (your time). When you do, you'll enjoy a feast from God and His Word!

Do something—So develop a plan, remembering (once again) that *something is better than nothing*. The important thing is to do something. Keep a record of your time with God for your own encouragement and accountability. I remember picking up my record one day, thinking, "It's only been a few days, Lord," and discovering it had actually been two weeks since I had done "something"! Don't be like I was. Have a plan to do something... and follow your plan.

Spiritual Growth Blesses Others

As Jesus grew, He also "increased...in favor with God and

men" (Luke 2:52). Try these three ways to improve your relationships with people.

Mind your mind—It's unavoidable. Your actions will reveal your attitude toward people. That's the message of yet another proverb: "For as he thinks in his heart, so is he" (Proverbs 23:7). Thoughts that are critical, negative, harmful, and jealous not only go against God's Word (Philippians 4:8), but they spawn actions that are critical, negative, harmful, and jealous. So train yourself to think loving, positive, sweet thoughts when it comes to other people.

Mind your mouth—Our relationships with people are enhanced when we follow in the steps of the Proverbs 31 woman who "opens her mouth with wisdom, and on her tongue is the law of kindness" (Proverbs 31:26). If her thoughts weren't wise or kind, her mouth was shut!

Mind your manners—The Number One way to be pleasing to God and approved by man is to be the servant of all. Our servant assignment from God is to give honor and preference to one another (Romans 12:10). Regarding others as more important than yourself gives you the mind and manner of Christ (Philippians 2:4-5).

You and I are to focus away from self and outward to others. We are to become other-oriented. To do this, as mundane as it sounds, we have to train ourselves to, for instance, stop talking about ourselves (and our children) and instead ask about the other person. We may also have to learn some good manners because love has good manners (1 Corinthians 13:5).

I love what Anne Ortlund says. First she writes, "There are two kinds of personalities in this world, and you are one of the two.

People can tell which, as soon as you walk into a room: your attitude says either 'Here I am' or 'There you are.'" Then she illustrates the latter by describing "a Hawaiian woman who strings a number of leis early each Sunday morning, not for anyone in particular! Then she comes to church praying, 'Lord, who needs my leis today? A newcomer? Someone discouraged? Lead me to the right people.'"[2]

Are you a "There you are" person, looking around for how you can encourage someone with God's love? He can make it happen as you let Him grow you into a woman after His heart.

Heart Response

How joyous! As Christian women, you and I are filled with all spiritual blessings (Ephesians 1:3). We are filled with the goodness of God (Galatians 5:22-23) and the Spirit of God (Galatians 4:6). We are also gifted for ministry (1 Corinthians 12:7-11; Romans 12:6-8). Now that we have been filled, God wants us to share those blessings with others, to invest our lives in other hearts, to give away His blessings, to pass them on. That, dear friend, is why you and I must be about the business of spiritual growth.

Because spiritual growth is grounded in Jesus Christ and empowered by His Spirit, I must ask you, "Is Jesus your Savior? Does He live in your heart?" After all, His presence is what makes you a woman after God's heart! Do you enjoy the assurance of eternal life? God has promised that "as many as received Him, to them He gave the right to become children of God, even to those who believe in His name" (John 1:12) and that "whoever believes in Him should not perish but have everlasting life" (John 3:16).

As a member of the family of God, you've also been given the mind of Christ (1 Corinthians 2:16). Are you purposefully filling your mind with knowledge from God's Word, knowledge you can give away to others? Does your body belong to God, to be groomed, cared for, and disciplined for maximum usefulness and His glory? And are you nurturing love for others—thinking, speaking, and acting toward them as Christ would?

God calls you to love Him, first and foremost, with all your heart, soul, strength, and mind (Luke 10:27) and to allow that rich love you enjoy in Him to overflow into your family, into your neighbors, into the lives of others (Luke 10:27). That's why a heart strengthened by spiritual growth in Him is so very important.

18

A Heart Enriched by Joy in the Lord

Be filled with all the fullness of God.
EPHESIANS 3:19

One Sunday morning I stopped on the church patio to talk to a long-time acquaintance. For the 30 years I attended that church, Sharon helped women like me grow in the things of the Lord and live out His priorities. Sharon has been a faithful Titus 2:3 older woman and mentor—a blessing to many.

As we talked that morning, she seemed electric—lit up, sparks flying, flowing and sizzling with live juice. Everything about Sharon that day evidenced both the vital life she lives in the Savior and her wholehearted pursuit of continued growth in Him. I can still picture her broad, brilliant smile and her eyes bright with inner energy. Uncontainably excited, she involuntarily punctuated her message with gestures and waves.

What was she so excited about? Well, Sharon was looking forward to hearing a very special speaker the next day. She could hardly wait, and judging by her exhilaration, I bet she didn't sleep that night! Her words tumbled out as she explained that she had already attended a weekend workshop led by this scholar and that it had been the most exciting weekend of her life, the most stimulating thing she'd ever done. This teacher had taken Sharon to new depths in God's Word, in her understanding of His ways, and in her ministry. As she talked, I knew I was in the presence of a woman who was growing in both the knowledge and love of her Lord. No wonder she was so happy and excited! No wonder she had so much to give to others! No wonder I felt blessed by her ministry of refreshment.

Everyone who gets close to these women receives something from the fullness of their lives. My deepest desire and prayer for you is that you will be this kind of woman.

Another woman like Sharon at this same church was a reader. I never saw her without a book resting on top of the Bible she always carries. Every time we spoke, she would ask, "Oh Elizabeth, have you read this book? It's a must!" And off we would go into a wonderful discussion of her latest find and why that particular book was so important to us as Christians. I was blessed by her ministry of refreshment too.

I hope you get a sense of how stimulating these women are and how they spurred me on in my own spiritual growth. These two women after God's own heart are alive and growing. There's an infectiousness about their lives and hearts that never fails to challenge and motivate me. It is impossible for me to leave their presence unchanged. The joy they gained from their growth in the Lord shines forth, and everyone who gets close to these women receives something from the fullness of their lives.

Even more than hoping you get a sense of women like these, I hope that God has placed some of these women in your life. But my deepest desire and prayer for you (and for myself too!) is that you will *be* this kind of woman. As God grows you into a woman after His heart, you will never lack for His joy or a fulfilling ministry for His kingdom!

In the preceding chapter, we began to plan for a life of spiritual growth that would lead to ministry to others. After all, as my mentor shared repeatedly with me, when nothing is coming in, nothing can go out. If, then, you and I are to have an effective ministry to others, we must first be filled. What can you do to be filled with all the fullness of God so that He can use you in ministry? Here are a few suggestions.

Spiritual Growth Is Aided by Discipleship

God's ideal plan for us as His women—and another aspect of His job assignment for us—is that we teach other women the "good things" we've been learning, that we mentor or disciple them, that we pass on all that God has taught us (Titus 2:3-4).

The word *discipleship* can call to mind a variety of scenarios. Most often we equate discipleship with one-on-one, weekly meetings with another woman for years on end. That would be wonderful, but for most people that is neither a reality nor even a possibility. We can, however, choose from some enriching alternatives if we really want to grow.

Classes are ours for the taking. Churches in every town offer Bible studies and Bible classes. Correspondence courses are also available.[1] All you and I have to do is enroll, do the work, and let God grow us.

Books offer another avenue for growth and help you develop skills for ministering to women. Like this book, most of my books (see the list in the back of this book) contain study questions or have companion growth and study guides available for personal study, growth, and discipleship.

Counsel from fellow Christians is also a valid form of discipleship. If you're having a problem, ask a trusted and godly person—and you'll receive God's perspective and the prayer support you need. Even if you're unable to attend any classes or meet with a mentor right now, you can always ask for counsel.

Interviewing other Christian women is one of my favorite means of growth and discipleship. When God sent a godly, older woman to my church, I took one look at her busy life and saw clearly that she would never be able to commit to a series of discipleship sessions with me. So I made a list of all the questions I wanted to ask her and set up an appointment. We met just that one time, but those two precious hours she gave me were life changing! Much of my philosophy of ministry and many of the things I teach (including my five fat files) are a direct result of that one blessed time in her presence, drinking in her wisdom.

Observation is another biblical means of growth. After all, "the hearing ear and the seeing eye, the LORD has made them both" (Proverbs 20:12). So make sure you are watching, watching, watching! It's a great way to learn. In fact, Bible teacher Carole Mayhall says one way to learn how to love and demonstrate respect and support your husband is to watch other women. When it comes to admiring your husband, for instance, "keep a list of how other women show admiration for their husbands."[2]

Watch, learn, write down what you learn, and then try those new behaviors yourself.

Reading plays an important role in spiritual growth. Of course, the primary book to read is your Bible. There you'll find God's direct teaching. Beyond God's Word, read the books of the women I've been mentioning throughout this book and others like them who have put into print for us their mentoring programs, their counsel, and their observations. When we read such books, we are discipled.

If you're not quite convinced, consider these thoughts about the value of reading:

- Mrs. Billy Graham told her daughters, "Keep reading and you'll be educated."[3]

- Don't forget to focus your reading on the areas of your five fat files! "The most important key to reading effectiveness can be summed up in one word—selectivity."[4]

- "Don't read at random—only what relates to your total life goals."[5]

- "One characteristic common to every effective person is that they are avid readers."[6]

- "Reading is the best way to gain knowledge…. [But] only 5% of the people living in the U.S. will either buy or read a book this year."[7]

If you're thinking, "But I don't have *time* to read! How could I with all these job assignments from God?" or "Wait a minute—books cost money!" a wise first step would be a sober evaluation of how you're living your life. It's easy to think you don't have time to read, but the simple act of carrying a book everywhere you go gets many books read. I used to set my timer and read for just five minutes a day. That approach also gets many books read.

As for the money, it's also easy to think you can't afford books. An option for many people is checking out books from your church library. But you may have the funds to build a library without knowing it. Did you know that the average household spends more than $50 a month (some even up to $200 a month!) for cable television service? How about spending the amount you spend for cable TV on edifying Christian books that stimulate spiritual growth? Have a book budget that matches your cable fees. Those TV programs will become less enjoyable next to life-giving books that enrich your spiritual growth.

Spiritual Growth Is Aided by Goals

I'm in the midst of preparing a Saturday seminar about setting and reaching goals. Needless to say, I am thrilled to be talking about something that helps guide me every day! I can't imagine a day (or a life) without goals. Goals give me a target. As I rise each morning and take aim at my day, the arrow I shoot may wobble and weave, but at least it's in flight and headed some-where. The arrow may miss the bull's eye, falling a little short or sometimes even quite wide of the goal, but at least it was going—*I* was going—somewhere. Just as goals help us in the day to day, goals are definitely an aid when it comes to our spiritual growth. Here's how.

Goals provide focus—It's definitely true that if you aim at noth-ing, you'll hit it every time. So when I was a mom with preschool-ers, I aimed at something—reading one book a year. I asked myself, "If I could read only one book this year, what would it be?" I picked Edith Schaeffer's book *What Is a Family?* Reading that one book when our children were young helped me determine the road I wanted our family to head down. I read it in bits and pieces, remembering that *something is better than nothing*. I set a goal—and reached it. And that one book I set out to read went straight into my heart—and my life. It was so powerful and helpful that I chose to read it again...and again. As time—and years—went by, my list of books grew to include a variety of other titles centered around my own personal five fat files, all of which have contributed to my personal and spiritual growth and to my ministry to others.

Goals provide an opportunity for specific measurement—Setting goals that are specific helps you move forward in the direction you want to go. So when it comes to making goals for yourself, stay away from the vague. For example, the goal "to be a godly woman" or "to walk with God" is honorable but hard to measure. It's far better to be specific. Answer the question "What does a godly woman *do?*" and let your answer give you specific and measurable behaviors (i.e., Bible study, prayer time). Write down steps you can actually take toward those behaviors (baby steps count!) and mark them off as you accomplish them. I'm often asked about my writing, including questions like "How do you do it?" and "What must I do to write a book?" My answer is always the same. I have a goal to write five pages each day. Now that's specific. There's nothing vague about that.

Goals provide encouragement—When a week, or month, or year is over, do you ever wonder, "Wow, what did I do? Where did it go?" I know I used to mourn the end of each year, wondering what I had to show for the passage of time, for a *whole* year. But as I began to write down specific, measurable goals and keep track of my progress in my planner, I could see firsthand the growth that had taken place, the number of books that had been read, the variety of classes and seminars taken, the audiences I had shared God's truths with, the books written, the number of family reunions and birthdays celebrated and babies added to our expanding family, even the pounds lost and a year's worth of efforts at physical fitness. Believe me, as you keep track daily of your efforts and God's grace, you will be able to celebrate the progress made, and give God thanks.

Spiritual Growth Depends on Choices

Once you've settled on some specific goals, you'll have to continually make the right choices if you are to reach those goals. What kinds of choices?

Choices based on priorities—To reach the goals you set for your spiritual growth, you'll have to choose between working on a Bible course, taking a theology class, reading a book, meeting with a mentor...or another luncheon outing, shopping (again) in the mall, watching still more TV, attending another church social, or working on a craft. Filling yourself up with spiritual things so that growth occurs and your life is a river of refreshment to many requires many tough choices.

Choices based on goals—Once you've decided to spend time on your spiritual growth, you still have to choose which project—and your five fat files can guide you. You'll also want to consider your spiritual gifts. These two guides will help you aim at the best choice.

Spiritual Growth Requires Time

God will honor the time we commit to learning more about

Him, the time we find, redeem, save, allow, and schedule for our spiritual growth. An image from Scripture (an image I love) encourages me here. The prophet Isaiah wrote, "Those who wait on the LORD shall...mount up with wings like eagles" (Isaiah 40:31). The time we spend in solitude with our Bible and our prayer list, our secret life spent with our heavenly Father, is time spent waiting upon the Lord. Then, in the fullness of time, in God's perfect timing, there is the mounting up, the taking flight like that eagle. We are able to soar because we've been with the Lord—as the lives of many heroes of the Bible illustrate.

- Moses was the adopted son of Pharaoh's daughter and, as such, experienced every known privilege for 40 years. But then God took him into the desert to be a shepherd, a nobody, for the next 40 years of his life (Exodus 3:1). After those 40 years of God preparing him, Moses burst on the scene with signs, wonders, miracles, and faithful service to God (Exodus 3–14).

- Potiphar was the captain of the guard for Pharaoh, and Joseph served ten years as master of Potiphar's household (Genesis 39). But one day Joseph found himself in prison, a nobody, forgotten as the days and months rolled by. Then, after two or three years, which God used to prepare him for leadership, Joseph burst on the scene, helped save his people, and served as second in command over the entire known world (Genesis 41).

- John the Baptist was another of God's nobodies. For 30 years he lived in the wilderness, wearing animal skins and eating locusts and wild honey (Matthew 3:4; Luke 1:80). After those 30 years of preparation, John burst on the scene preaching like no man ever had, preaching so powerfully

that his listeners thought he was the Messiah (Luke 3:15)!
John's ministry lasted no longer than one brief year, yet it
demanded lengthy spiritual preparation.

- Paul was a terrible somebody who persecuted Christians.
  But then one day he was dramatically converted from
  Christian-hater to Christian—and he disappeared into the
  Arabian desert for three years (Galatians 1:17-18). After
  those three years, during which God prepared him for an
  amazing and far-reaching ministry, Paul burst on the scene,
  preaching, teaching, and working signs and miracles.

- And then there is Jesus. As God in flesh, He was never a
  nobody. But He too put in His time in obscurity, away
  from the crowds, involved in the mundane. According to
  God's plan, Jesus spent time as a child in Galilee with a
  family, time inside a carpenter's workshop, and time in
  the wilderness for 40 days of prayer and fasting (Matthew
  4:1-11). And then one day Jesus burst on the scene exhib-
  iting the power and glory of God in action! But after 30
  years of preparation, His earthly ministry lasted for only
  three short years.

God's perspective on time is different from ours, and we may
question His use of time. We may be tempted to think that quiet,
hidden time with Him doesn't count—that it doesn't show, it
doesn't matter, and no one cares. After all, nobody sees it. There's
no glory, no splash, no attention given to those weeks, months,
years of waiting on God. No one sees us read and study God's
empowering Word. No one is present to watch us memorize and
meditate on God's life-changing truths. God alone sees us on
bended knee in the heart-wrenching work of prayer, work He
uses to prepare us for ministry.

But then, just like the heroes of the Bible and just like our Savior Himself, one day we are prepared. When the timing is right, when the opportunity for ministry presents itself, we too mount up with wings like an eagle—ready to do God's work! We are then privileged to live out the saying that success

> *Treat yourself to a private retreat and wait on the Lord. Let God prepare you to mount up with wings like an eagle so that you one day burst on the scene in vital ministry to His people!*

comes when preparation meets opportunity. God is responsible for presenting the opportunities—in His time, place, and manner—but we are responsible for cooperating with His efforts to prepare us.

And that preparation happens when we spend time alone with our Lord. Good comes out of that time. In fact, for good reason, solitude has been called "the school of genius." It's also true that "most of the world's progress has come out of…loneliness."[8] So clear your calendar. Set aside time to place yourself before God so He can bring about spiritual growth in you. Treat yourself to a private retreat and wait on the Lord. Let God prepare you to mount up with wings like an eagle so that you one day burst on the scene in vital ministry to His people!

Spiritual Growth Results in Ministry

The importance of your spiritual growth—the main point of this section—is summed up in the statement, *You cannot give away what you do not possess.* Involvement in ministry requires that you be a full vessel—as my friend Karen (another Karen!) will show you.

As a mother with two little boys at home, Karen desired to

be a full vessel. So she began waiting on the Lord. She set up her five fat files and began to read and read and read(!) on one of her selected files, *the spiritual development of children.*

Soon Karen's older son went off to kindergarten for three hours a day. At the end of the year, when the teacher was setting up "graduation" exercises, she asked Karen to give a message on imparting spiritual truth to your children. With that invitation, a prepared Karen burst on the scene—and had a hundred people hear what she had learned.

Because Karen had faithfully waited on the Lord and put herself in a position where He could fill her and grow her, she possessed something she could give away. Everywhere she went, her lips and life spoke of the fullness that was being gained in private. She was so enriched and excited about what she was learning that it spilled out of her heart. Because the springs of her heart were being fed from an underground source, she had an excitement that refreshed others, and a natural overflow and ministry resulted.

And I'm sure you're a lot like Karen. As a woman after God's own heart, you undoubtedly want to know God and His Word. You want to make the choices He would have you make. You also desire God's power and imprint to clearly be on your life. Your heart beats with His out of concern for others. And you want to spend your life trying to live out God's purpose for you. That's what Karen longed for, so she set about filling herself up.

Spiritual Growth: Experiencing the Joy of the Lord

In your mind, picture a real woman you admire and then describe her as I described Sharon at the beginning of this chapter.

Most likely, the woman you admire is stimulating, challenging, energetic, and joyful. She is growing and fresh, excited and exciting, learning and willing to share what she is learning. She motivates you, and you love to be in her presence. She has nothing to fear, and you never hear her sigh or see signs that she's bored. For her, life is never dull!

Such a woman—and I hope you know at least one—is probably involved in and committed to spiritual growth. She has spent time with God and been filled by Him, so when she's in public, she can't help but share her love for Jesus. She can't help but share the joy of knowing Him and walking with Him. He has filled her heart to overflowing, enabling her to offer a ministry of refreshment to other people. As you watch these Proverbs 31 women dip into the reservoir created by their time of preparation with God and as you listen to their enthusiasm for life and for the Lord, you must admit that you are in the presence of a woman who truly knows His joy. That's where real joy comes from—time spent alone with the Lord as He enriches you and prepares you for the ministry of helping others.

Heart Response

You are blessed indeed if you know one of these joyful, enriched women who have responded to God's call on their lives. You will be even more blessed if you accept the invitation to do likewise. So take a moment and wait upon the Lord as you consider these questions:

- Exactly how am I spending my precious God-given time and energy? Am I wasting it on choices that have no heavenly value or am I making the good, better, and best choices?

- Do I acknowledge the value—the necessity—of time spent in preparation?

- Is allowing God to prepare me for ministry even a goal of mine? Or am I letting time—and life—slip away unused, uninvested in eternity?

God has done His part—He has saved you (2 Timothy 1:9), given you eternal life (1 John 5:11), blessed you with all spiritual blessings (Ephesians 1:3), gifted you for spiritual ministry (1 Corinthians 12:11), and prepared a place for you in heaven (John 14:2). And now He calls you to do your part—to catch His vision, to set aside time, to make growth in Him a goal, to spend time and energy so that He can prepare you for ministry, and to trust Him to provide you with opportunities to minister to and enrich His people out of the overflow of your own joy-filled and enriched life.

19

A Heart That Shows It Cares

Be steadfast, immovable,
always abounding in the work of the Lord,
knowing that your labor is not in vain in the Lord.
1 CORINTHIANS 15:58

When my daughter Courtney returned from her honeymoon, Jim and Katherine and I had exactly one week to help her pack and say goodbye as she and her Paul put their wedding gifts on a sea freighter and flew to the island of Kauai where Paul was a teacher. Hawaii is a long way from Los Angeles, and having a family member that far away was a real adjustment for Jim and Katherine and me. "Oh, well," all of us on the mainland thought, "we'll just *have* to visit them!" So Jim and I, along with Katherine and her husband, Paul, started planning a trip to Hawaii. (Yes, each of my daughters married a Paul!)

Five months later we flew to Maui for a long-awaited reunion. The four of us met Paul and Courtney and began a wonderful

Thanksgiving holiday together as a family. One of our sightseeing ventures took us on the famous Road to Hana where the Maui highway ends. Yes, we suffered our share of lightheadedness and car sickness as the road snaked around and around for 30 miles (and five hours!), but at the end of the road was a breathtaking view of the Seven Sacred Pools.

These seven pools had been formed in the rocks and lava beds by rain rushing down the mountainsides toward the Pacific Ocean. Originating high above in altitudes unseen because of the ever-present rain clouds, the fresh water fell to the ground. First it filled the highest pool. When that top pool was full, the still falling rain caused its contents to overflow and cascade into another pool down the mountain. As soon as that second pool filled up, it too overflowed…into another one further down the slope…and another…and another…until the last and final pool poured its contents into the immensity of God's sea.

Reflecting on God's Plan

As I stood with my family looking at (and photographing) this wondrous handiwork of God, I thought of the life you and I are seeking to live as God's women. These seven pools illustrate for us the fullness we can enjoy—and the far-reaching impact we can have—as we live according to God's plan.

Picture again that top pool, high on that mountain, veiled in a cloudy mist, hidden from the sight of others. Like that pool, you and I enjoy our hidden life with God, the private life we nurture in Him. Unseen by others, you and I are filled by God's Spirit as we dwell in His presence and drink from His Word. In that holy mist He replenishes our dry souls until we are filled with His goodness. Then that fullness overflows down into the next pool, the hearts of the people nearest and dearest to us— our husbands.

Then it happens again. Still high on the mountain, we share with our husbands from the fullness of our relationship with God, tending and nurturing that most important human relationship and developing the qualities that God desires in us wives. God grows in us a servant spirit and a heart filled with love that evidence themselves with that man. Soon this crystal pool of love swells until it cascades into the hearts of our children.

Yes, the hearts of our children are the next pool our love and energy are to fill. If God gives us children, He entrusts them to our care, to be loved and taught and trained and filled with the knowledge of Him. All that God has filled us with and all the blessings that spring from a love-filled, Christ-centered marriage overflow to refresh and supply the tender hearts of our dear children.

> *When we are faithful to follow after God's heart—when we tend and nurture each aspect of life as He instructs—the ministry He uses us in can have an impact beyond measure.*

The bounteous richness of our relationships with God, husband, and children then splashes into the next pool, filling our home with God's love and the beauty of family. The springs of God's love and care feed the spiritual life, family life, love life there in our refuge. Soon, too, this pool is filled to overflowing....

And then the waters rush down to the next level of need, satisfying our soul's desires. That rapidly filling lagoon is where dreams are dreamed, where we get a glimpse of what God wants you and me to do for Him and His people. Here we feel passionately that we want our lives to count. Here we desire to serve others according to God's purpose for us. Having been filled from the pools higher up the mountain, now we plunge in. We submerge ourselves in this fresh pool of knowledge, discipline, and training until, sure enough, the water level rises to the brink and surges beyond its limits, pouring forth into God's limitless ocean of ministry and service that builds His people up.

From our vantage point, as we reflect on how God might use us, we are silenced, awestruck. Now we understand! His ways are wise, and His ways work. When we are faithful to follow after God's heart—when we tend and nurture each aspect of life as He instructs—the ministry He uses us in can have an impact beyond measure.

Again, my heart sister, can you see it? Those seven pools show us how God can use our lives most effectively for His kingdom. God wants us to first touch those closest to us, but He can also use us to touch the multitudes. Having addressed the importance of spiritual growth, now I want us to look at how the water in that pool spills out into God's ocean of ministry. Let's consider some ways every Christian woman can influence the lives of others— countless others—for eternity. There is nothing listed here that you and I cannot do with God's help.

Learn to Reach Out

Again and again Jesus tells us to give—to give to everyone (Luke 6:30); to give hoping for nothing in return (verse 35); to give in the generous way God, who is kind to the unthankful and evil, gives (verse 35); and to care for others by giving (verse 38). You and I can learn to give in this way, to overflow with care for all others. Here are a few ideas.

Your presence and sometimes a single touch are worth a thousand words—When it comes to reaching out, remember this principle of ministry: Your very presence is a source of comfort. You may not have the exact words to say or the perfect Scripture to share.

But in many if not most situations, your touch can bring comfort far greater than words.

Be a giver—Just as you and I learned with our husbands and children, we can give the smile, the greeting, the warm question, the touch, the hug, and the name (always use the person's name!).

Be bold—Be bold and give to the people God places in your path. If, however, you find yourself avoiding a certain person, ask God to show you why. Sin in our hearts—hearts meant to overflow with care for others—keeps us from being confident in our relationships. So find out what is going on—or not going on—in your heart that's hindering your ministry. Then go a step further and decide what you will say the next time you see that person. Actively search for him or her and *give* the warm, friendly greeting you planned. With a heart clean before God, you should have nothing to hide, nothing to withhold. Learn to reach out to the people you meet up with every day.

Become a generous soul—Don't just give, but give liberally, cheerfully, bountifully, hilariously, extra, above and beyond (2 Corinthians 9:6-7)! "The generous soul will be made rich," Proverbs 11:25 informs us. But becoming that "generous soul" can be a process, and I've been in process for decades.

My husband, Jim, is this wonderfully generous soul who gives everything away. He's given away our cars, our groceries, our money, our savings, his suits, and our home to be used by others when we are away. I'm learning to be more generous, and one important lesson came when a couple from our home church showed me what it's like to be on the receiving end of such generosity. While we were missionaries in Singapore, they came for a visit. As we shopped the streets and harbor of that world-port city, Billie bought two of everything—and then gave the second of each (batik clothes, Christmas ornaments, china) to me when she left! What a joy to me—and what a privilege that you and I can give that kind of joy to others by giving generously.

It's been by God's blessing, but over the decades I've grown in this grace of giving. I remember growing to the point of conviction over my lack of generosity that I made "Giving" a category on my daily prayer list. In other words, I went after this Christlike character quality and trait God calls us to. I began to regularly ask God, "Who can I give to today? Who, Lord, is in need? How can I bless others with what You have blessed me with?" Yes, financial giving was part of what I was acting on. But I'm not just referring to money. No, our giving reaches into every part of our soul and our possessions. You and I have groceries in the pantry, clothes or baby items someone else could use, books that can encourage and edify others. We just need hearts that are open and generous.

Now, can you imagine how shocked I was when Jim and I were interviewed together on a Valentine's Day radio program where Jim was asked what he admired most about me...and he replied, "Elizabeth's generous heart. She is a very giving person." By God's grace and transforming power, *He* had worked that miracle in my heart...and He can do the same in yours.

Determine to withhold nothing—Proverbs 3:27 exhorts us, "Do not withhold good from those to whom it is due, when it is in the power of your hand to do so." What are some of the good things "in the power of your hand"? Praise, encouragement, thanks, a greeting, kindness, good deeds, and a note of appreciation are a few of the good things we hold. And you and I *choose* whether or not we will share these blessings.

I am encouraged each time I remember the first Bible lesson I ever taught. Our former pastor's wife hesitated and then made her way up the aisle afterwards. Struggling inside, she finally said, "I've been asking the Lord if I should say anything to you because I don't want this to go to your head or puff you up—but you are a good teacher!" Believe me, I will rarely suffer from overconfidence! My tendency is toward the other end of the scale, toward inadequacy, inferiority, and inability. But this esteemed woman chose not to withhold the good—those words of encouragement—when it was in the power of her hand (and heart) to give it. Let's make that same choice!

Learn to Look Out

I love the tender heart of the shepherd Jesus describes in Luke 15. When one of his 100 sheep was missing, he left the 99 and went looking for the one that was lost (verses 3-6). God cares for you and me this way, and He wants us to care for others this way too. Here are some tips for getting started.

Develop a "generous eye"—Solomon said, "He who has a generous eye will be blessed, for he gives of his bread to the poor" (Proverbs 22:9). I like to think of a generous eye as being like the eyes of God, which "run to and fro throughout the whole earth" (2 Chronicles 16:9). When I go into public places, I intentionally look for wounded sheep—and, believe me, they are there. I've found women in the ladies' room crying, sitting on the church patio weeping, standing behind our prayer room door sobbing. One night during church I sat beside a woman who cried for one-and-a-half hours! I could hardly wait for my pastor to finish praying so I could ask her, "Can I do *anything* to help you? Can I pray with you? Can I get you something? Would you like to talk?" People all around us need a tender word—or more. (Do you see why you and I must be developing and overcoming selfish tendencies? That way we can give to others.)

Be direct—Whenever you see a person in need, be direct. Walk straight up to the wounded sheep and see what she needs and what you can do. Don't hope someone else comes along. Don't run looking for the pastor. God has allowed *you* to find this person in need. Now allow *your* heart to overflow with care.

Go to Give

Missionary and martyr Jim Elliot once said, "Wherever you are, be all there. Live to the hilt every situation you believe to be the will of God."[1] I keep these words in mind whenever I attend any church or ministry event, and I go expecting God to use me. Here's an overview of my approach—and I encourage you to make it yours.

Be all there—Before I go to an event, I pray that I will go to give—to reach out, to look out, to be direct, to withhold nothing. Then, as I go, I put my thought life on guard. While I'm at Bible study, I don't want to be thinking about what I'm going to fix for dinner that night. During my pastor's message, I don't want to be planning my week. I don't want to be concerned about what happened before I got there or what will happen after the event. I want to be all there.

Live to the hilt!—Not only do I want to be all there, but I want to also live each moment to the hilt. And I like the advice of Anne Ortlund, a wife of a pastor. She encourages women to be "hanger-arounders."[2] As long as you're there, as long as you've given an evening or a morning to an event or Bible study or worship service, give totally. Try to reach out to as many sheep as you can. Minister to as many people as you can in as many ways as you can.

Divide and conquer—Agree with your closest girlfriends, mother, or daughter *not* to sit together, walk together, share coffee time together, or visit. Instead share the commitment to divide and conquer. Remember, you came to give! Your family and closest friends have greater access to your life, plenty of one-on-one time with you in private, so why should they also have all your public time? They can talk to you later. One friend and I have made a pact that when we find ourselves gravitating toward each other, one of us will announce, "Come on! Let's go touch some sheep!"

And one more word about going to give. You'll find yourself doing a lot of receiving—you'll find yourself quite blessed—as you let God use you in this way!

Develop Your Prayer Life

Have you noticed how again and again in this book we come back to prayer? A woman after God's own heart is a woman who prays. Her heart naturally overflows in prayer as well as care. And since praying for people is a powerful way to care for them, you and I should want to join with God in a ministry of prayer, a ministry that makes a huge difference in people's lives. Learn—as I have—from J. Sidlow Baxter's story about how he developed his prayer life.

> I found that there was an area of me that did not want to pray...[and] there was a part of me that did. The part that didn't was the emotions, and the part that did was the intellect and the will....

[So] I said to my will: "Will, are you ready for prayer?"
And Will said, "Here I am, I'm ready." So I said, "Come
on, Will, we will go."

So Will and I set off to pray. But the minute we turned
our footsteps to go and pray all my emotions began to talk:
"We're not coming, we're not coming, we're not coming."
And I said to Will, "Will, can you stick it?" And Will
said, "Yes, if you can." So Will and I, we dragged off those
wretched emotions and we went to pray, and stayed an
hour in prayer.

If you had asked me afterwards, Did you have a good
time, do you think I could have said yes? A good time? No,
it was a fight all the way.

What I would have done without the companionship of
Will, I don't know. In the middle of the most earnest inter-
cessions I suddenly found one of the principal emotions
way out on the golf course, playing golf. And I had to run
to the golf course and say, "Come back."...It was exhaust-
ing, but we did it.

The next morning came. I looked at my watch and
it was time. I said to Will, "Come on, Will, it's time for
prayer." And all the emotions began to pull the other way
and I said, "Will, can you stick it?" And Will said, "Yes, in
fact I think I'm stronger after the struggle yesterday morning." So Will and I went in again.

The same thing happened. Rebellious, tumultuous,
uncooperative emotions. If you had asked me, "Have you
had a good time?" I would have had to tell you with tears,
"No, the heavens were like brass. It was a job to concentrate. I had an awful time with the emotions."

This went on for about two-and-a-half weeks. But Will

and I stuck it out. Then one morning during that third week I looked at my watch and I said, "Will, it's time for prayer. Are you ready?" And Will said, "Yes, I'm ready."

And just as we were going in I heard one of my chief emotions say to the others, "Come on, fellows, there's no use wearing ourselves out: they'll go on whatever we do."...

Suddenly one day [weeks later] while Will and I were pressing our case at the throne of the heavenly glory, one of the chief emotions shouted "Hallelujah!" and all the other emotions suddenly shouted, "Amen!" For the first time [all of me was involved] in the exercise of prayer.[3]

Prayer isn't easy! It's definitely a discipline, but it's also a ministry that flows from a full heart. Three decisions can help you place yourself before God so He can fill your heart with concern for others.

Determine a time—Just as Mr. Baxter looked at his watch and said, "It is time," we too ensure that the ministry of prayer takes place by establishing a set time for it. Schedule a time, turn off the phone, leave other things undone, and sit or kneel down... and pray.

> *By setting a time, determining a place, and having a plan, nothing and no one will be forgotten. Everything and everyone will be covered when you pray.*

Determine a place—Choose a location that is quiet, where you can be alone to "press *your* case at the throne of the heavenly glory."

Determine a plan—Use a notebook to help you organize

your ministry of prayer. In my notebook, I first list everyone I want to pray for. Then I decide how often I want (or time and urgency allows) to pray for each one. Some are daily (including my "enemies"—Luke 6:27-28), but most are weekly. Finally I assign a specific day to each category. I also keep a page for "special requests" and another for extended family members. Create as many pages and categories as you need to pray for the people God has placed in your life to care for.[4]

By setting a time, determining a place, and having a plan, nothing and no one will be forgotten. Everything and everyone will be covered when you pray. These practical steps enable us to fulfill God's desire that we be "praying always...with all perseverance and supplication for all the saints" (Ephesians 6:18).

Heart Response

Do you feel the mist on your face as you let God fill you? Are you aware of how full your heart is, the heart after God He has been growing in you while you read 19 chapters of this book? And do you sense how its overflow is tumbling and splashing into a sea of love for the people around you? It is a glorious experience to be filled to overflowing with the love of God and then to be used by Him!

I hope too that your heart is at rest and that you've found your deepest fulfillment in seeing how God extends His love to so many through you. First His love flows to those people closest to your heart, those people at home. Then His love moves on through you to invigorate and refresh countless others. As this happens, your gracious and generous God miraculously refills you, replacing and multiplying all that you selflessly give away to others.

As you consider this process, I pray that you are encouraged. Once you've tasted the blissful joy born of personal sacrifice (if you haven't already), I pray that your heart is filled with deep spiritual satisfaction and contentment. May you know beyond all doubt that your labor for the Lord is never in vain (1 Corinthians 15:58). And may you never grow weary of doing good, "for in due season [you] shall reap if [you] do not lose heart" (Galatians 6:9)! Ask God to give you a greater desire to serve Him and others. Go to Him for wisdom as you choose where and how to minister. And be sure you always make the time to fill your own heart so that you have something to give to others. Finally, look to God to give you strength for His work and a broader vision of the eternal value of serving Him and His people.

20

A Heart That Encourages

A good word makes [the heart] glad.
PROVERBS 12:25

Sitting in our Sunday school class, I listened and took notes as Jim continued his series on the "one anothers" in the New Testament. He was teaching about the ministries each of us Christians is to have to our fellow members of Christ's church. This particular Sunday Jim spoke on edifying one another—encouraging them, building them up, contributing positively to their lives, and benefiting them in some way.

Summarizing the lesson with a point of application, Jim challenged our class. He exhorted, "With every encounter, make it your aim that people are better off for having been in your presence. Try in every encounter to give something to the other person." I have never forgotten these words. What a great—and simple—way to positively influence the lives of other people. Everyone needs edification and encouragement, and we are free to offer that when we have hearts filled by God. Here are some hints for encouraging God's people.

Take Time to Be Filled

If you take time to sit at Jesus' feet and be filled by God's Spirit as you study the written Word, if you focus on overcoming internal obstacles to doing God's work, you will never lack for ministry. God's fullness in you will naturally overflow into the lives of others. I think immediately of two women who increased their ministry potential when they overcame their shyness.

Evangelist Corrie ten Boom had a problem with shyness. Determined to overcome it, she enrolled in a Dale Carnegie course so she could learn to talk to people. If she could talk to people, then she could witness to them about Jesus Christ. Developing herself in this way led to greater ministry.

You have more to give to your neighbor if you regularly place yourself before God and let Him grow you, strengthen you, transform you!

Mrs. Howard Hendricks is a pastor's wife who had a problem with shyness. Like Corrie ten Boom, Jeanne enrolled in a Dale Carnegie course and also a Toastmasters for Women to learn how to talk with people individually and in groups. Twice I've attended women's retreats where Mrs. Hendricks was the retreat speaker—speaking each time to more than 500 women. Developing herself led to more capable ministry.

Ministry and service to others is stimulated when we take the time to develop our skills and overcome our weaknesses— and that makes sense. After all, how much can a teacher teach, a counselor counsel, an administrator administrate? Only as far as each has grown! And each of us grows, each of us finds power and knowledge for overcoming personal weaknesses and for more effective ministry in Jesus Christ. And Jesus Himself said, "'You shall love the LORD your God with all your heart, with all your soul, with all your strength, and with all your mind,' and 'your neighbor as yourself'" (Luke 10:27). You have more to give to your neighbor if you regularly place yourself before God and let Him grow you, strengthen you, transform you!

Memorize Scriptures of Encouragement

Do you remember when we discussed "salting" our children with truths from the Bible? Well, children are not the only people in your life who need salt! You can have the ministry of salting—the ministry of encouragement—with everyone you meet. If you "let your speech always be with grace, seasoned with salt" (Colossians 4:6), you will never fail to better the lives of those you encounter. Your life and lips will offer refreshing encouragement to all who cross your path. Like our Messiah, you will be able to "speak a word in season to him who is weary" (Isaiah 50:4).

> *If you are faithful to commit to memory selected gems from God's Word, you'll suddenly find them adding real substance to your conversations.*

But, as we've seen before, we can't give away what we do not possess. So it's good to memorize some pertinent words of encouragement from the Bible to share with people in need. Knowing Scripture gives you "a word in season," something timely and appropriate to the situation.

Think of the Scripture passages you memorize as a surgeon's instruments. The last things I saw before I slipped into unconsciousness before my own surgery several years ago were two trays of such instruments, one on the surgeon's right and one on his left. I remember thinking, "Look at all those instruments! All sizes! All shapes! All kinds! And so many of them! Whatever he needs is right there—ready for any and every purpose!"

That's what the Scriptures you've memorized become in the hands of God—instruments ready for any and every purpose. Whatever the need (in your own life as well as in the lives of those you talk with), every verse you know by heart is available, sharp, and ready for God to use to encourage a weary soul.

If you are faithful to commit to memory selected gems from God's Word, you'll suddenly find them adding real substance to your conversations. This is another natural overflow from a full heart—in this case, a heart filled to overflowing with God's Word. You'll find the content of the notes you write and the telephone calls you make taking on added depth. Your visits with others will become more meaningful as you share God's powerful truths and promises. In fact, because your heart is full of Scripture, you'll no longer be satisfied with meaningless, trivial conversations. Sharing God's Word will take your talks with others to deeper levels.

In case you're thinking, "But I can't memorize Scripture! I've tried, and it just won't work for me," I was recently in a friend's home whose pet parrot sang "The Star-Spangled Banner" in its entirety for me. As I stood there amazed at what I was hearing, I thought, *Well, if a parrot can learn "The Star-Spangled Banner," we human beings can all learn to memorize Scripture!* Think of the time it took for a bird to learn the melody and tune of such a complicated song. Surely you can learn a verse or two from God's Word. If you do, your filled heart will be a source of encouragement to many!

Make Phone Calls to Encourage

We are told in the Bible that "anxiety in the heart of man causes depression, but a good word makes it glad" (Proverbs 12:25), and you probably know that truth from experience. An easy way to encourage and make a heart glad is to reach out and touch someone by phone. I'm not talking about calling long lists of people or even making lengthy calls. A simple, quick call can do much to gladden the heart of the recipient.

I usually make these sunshine calls at about 5:30 in the afternoon. When my girls were at home, I would say to each one, "I have to make three phone calls. They won't take long, but I want to know if there's anything you need before I get on the phone." Speaking to Katherine and Courtney first conveyed to them their priority position in my heart over everyone else (including those I was calling). It also gave me the chance to take care of any of their needs before I got on the phone and to remind them that I wouldn't be available to them for a few minutes.

(And guess what? Today these years later, my two daughters are at the top of my list for making phone calls of encouragement. With seven little ones between them I know they need a good word now and then—even often! I know a familiar voice from someone who loves them can make their day...which is always busy and packed. I pray before I dial to be positive, energetic, uplifting. I pray to build them up, compliment them, remind them of their strengths, let them know how proud I am of them... and always express my respect for what good wives and moms they are. When they answer, the first thing I ask is, "Is this a good time to talk or would you like me to call you back?" And if they don't answer the phone, I leave a cheerful message that I'm thinking about them and will call again soon. In other words, I don't ask them to call me back. I've witnessed how hectic it can get in their homes, and they don't need one more thing—like "Return Mom's phone call" on their "to do" lists. My girls now live thousands of miles away on the east coast, but when they lived nearby I would also always ask, "How can I help you today? What needs to be done that I can do for you?"

Anyway, back to phoning others....When I call others, I say something like "I know you're about to eat—and so are we—but I haven't seen you lately, and I just had to give you a quick call and make sure you're all right." If there is a difficulty, I make an appointment to call back at a time when we can have a more lengthy and meaningful conversation. You and I can also reach out in this way to people recovering from illnesses or dealing with a crisis. The telephone offers us a very effective way to encourage others, and it takes very little effort. Most important to that ministry is a heart that cares!

When Jim pastored the senior citizens at our former church, I found that making phone calls was a simple way to encourage those in our class who were absent on Sundays. If they were ill or out of town they were thrilled that someone noticed, missed them, and checked up on them. My special friend Patty blesses me in the same way, leaving encouraging words on my answering machine when we haven't seen each other for a while. It always makes me smile to hear her message and know *someone* out there cares.

I use the internet too—24/7—as a tool for encouragement. How easy it is to sit down for a few seconds and dash off a few sentences to bolster a missionary on the other side of the world, a friend who has moved away, those in ministry at my church, a hurting woman....and, of course, my daughters.

Who can you share a smile with by phone or online?

Write Notes of Encouragement

Writing notes—again, by mail or email—to those who need encouragement is another way to share a good word that makes the heart glad (Proverbs 12:25). Again, when it came to the seniors Jim and I were shepherding, I would pray and ask God, "What can I—a young wife and mother—possibly give these saints? They have walked with You so long. They know You so well."

God was faithful to answer that plea from my heart. He showed me that I could write them encouraging notes. So when I took attendance each Sunday morning, I began noting who was absent, who was traveling, and who was ill. Later that afternoon at home, while the children napped and Jim and I relaxed, I wrote each of the missing sheep a note of encouragement. I just wanted to convey to them that we cared and were concerned as well as available—and that we looked forward to seeing them again soon.

The people I admire most in this area of note writing are those who set aside certain time slots in their day or week for the express purpose of writing notes and letters. It *is* a ministry! And if you're thinking again, "Oh, no! I'm already so busy. How can I add one more thing?" consider my simple approach. As I face a blank piece of notepaper, I tell myself, "Come on, Elizabeth, just three sentences!" Whether I'm writing to the sick, the bereaved, those in leadership, or a recent hostess, telling myself "Just three sentences!" gets me going.

> Sentence #1 conveys I miss you, I appreciate you, or I'm thinking of you.
>
> Sentence #2 lets readers know they are special to me and why.
>
> And sentence #3 says I'm praying for them and includes the verse I'm praying for them.

As you sit in bed or on a couch with your feet propped up, you can give this kind of encouragement to others out of your heart filled by God's love—and the recipients will be very blessed!

These days I try to carry with me a folder that contains the correspondence I need to answer, the names of those I need to thank in some way, and a liberal supply of notecards, envelopes, postcards, and stamps. I also carry my laptop computer, so that wherever I am—on a plane, in a hotel, waiting in an airport, relaxing at a conference center, waiting for my husband in the car, or sitting in the library, a coffee shop, or a pew at church a few minutes early—I can encourage others with a note. And so can you—in just three sentences!

Encourage Others Through Three Spiritual Gifts

When I read *Balancing the Christian Life* by theologian Charles Caldwell Ryrie, I discovered three more ministries that you and I—and all Christians—can have. In fact, as Dr. Ryrie pointed out, these three ministries are not only specific spiritual gifts, but they are commanded of all Christians. Dr. Ryrie describes them as "three of the [spiritual] gifts…probably all Christians could have and use if they would. They are ministering, giving, and showing mercy (Romans 12:7-8)."[1] Hear how Dr. Ryrie defines them:

> *Serving* is sometimes called help or ministering. "It is the basic ability to help other people, and there is no reason why every Christian cannot have and use this gift."
>
> *Mercy* is next. "Showing mercy is akin to the gift of ministering and involves succoring those who are sick or afflicted. 'Pure religion and undefiled before

God and the Father is this, to visit the fatherless and widows in their affliction' (James 1:27)."

Giving is another ministry you and I could—and should—be involved in. "Giving is the ability to distribute one's own money to others, and it is to be done with simplicity which means with no thought of return or gain for oneself in any way."[2]

Serving, mercy, and giving—each is a specific spiritual gift, but each is also commanded of us as Christians. *And* each was carried out and modeled for us by our dear Savior, in whose steps we are to follow. So commit now to kindle your efforts to serve, show mercy, and give—and thus fulfill the law of God and encourage His people.

Live Your Priorities

By living out your priorities you will teach and disciple many women—without saying a word. The best way to teach priorities to others is to model those priorities. After all—and this is another principle for us women after God's own heart—*one picture is worth a thousand words*. As we've discussed, God has given us such a picture in Proverbs 31:11-31. Here He paints a portrait of a woman living out her priorities. And have you ever noticed that none of her *words* are recorded? No, only her *works* survive.

By God's grace and in His power, you can encourage others just as this "wonder"ful woman encourages you. Simply concentrate on being who God wants you to be and doing what He wants you to do. Concentrate on mastering your priorities. Don't worry about organizing your thoughts, preparing a lesson, and getting up in front of a group. Just walk among the women at your church and in your neighborhood *doing* with all your heart what you are supposed to do.

Every Christian woman needs models and examples—and I am no different. I remember being a new Christian and going to church, looking for models. I carefully watched other Christian women. I observed how they behaved in church and even what they wore. Did they speak up in mixed groups? Did they pray out loud? I noted how they treated their husbands, how they showed respect, how they behaved as a couple in public. I also watched the moms with their children, noticing how they disciplined, the tone of voice they used when they spoke to their children, and even the expressions on their faces as they looked at their little ones. Nothing slipped by me because I knew I needed help!

> *Being what God wants you to be—being a woman after God's own heart—is a powerful ministry.*

As an experienced observer of other women, I know that *everything you do and don't do teaches*. Gossip may seem like a little thing, but when you don't gossip, you teach other women the beauty of obedience. When you say, "I'll have to ask my husband about that," you show other wives how to make their husbands a priority. When you plan your day around your children's schedules, you model for other moms respect and consideration for their children.

If you are in a phase of life that doesn't allow you to formally teach or lead or participate in a women's ministry, you're still teaching! Think about it this way—perhaps your very absence from those functions is teaching something about your priorities. Maybe some of the people who are in attendance shouldn't be there either.

Remember the quote I shared earlier? The wisdom goes like this: "We [must] say 'no' not only to things which are wrong and sinful, but to things pleasant, profitable, and good which would hinder and clog our grand duties and our chief work."[3] By now you are probably understanding more fully what your grand duties and chief work as a Christian woman, wife, mother, home manager, and worker in the church are. By now you know more clearly what God says is most important. Being what God wants you to be—being a woman after God's own heart—is a powerful ministry. Others can simply watch you and be encouraged in their own quest to follow God.

Heart Response

When you and I made our way through the section about our spiritual growth, we stretched ourselves. We set goals. We decided to do the work that growth requires. Our aim was to let God fill us up and prepare us for future ministry and service to others. Acknowledging that this would be hard but rewarding work, we forged ahead, increasing our knowledge and honing our skills.

Now consider the simplicity and ease of the ministries we've considered here!

✓ Writing a note
✓ Making a few phone calls
✓ Speaking words of grace
✓ Modeling God's priorities

Ministry is always a matter of the heart. If your heart is filled with a watchful concern for God's people, you will be privileged to refresh many souls in need of encouragement.

These are next to effortless. Each one, however, requires a heart filled with God's love and with sensitivity for others. Ministry is always a matter of the heart. *If* your heart is filled with a watchful concern for God's people, you will be privileged to refresh many souls in need of encouragement just like a rain cloud delivers much-needed moisture to a parched earth. I hope and pray your heart response to God will be to take the few moments these ministries call for and use them to share God's love with others.

Part 3

The Practice
of God's Priorities

21

A Heart That Seeks First Things First

Early will I seek You.
PSALM 63:1

Step back with me for a moment to the Seven Sacred Pools mentioned in chapter 19. Remember how they illustrate the beauty of God's plan for our life as women after His heart. Like those sparkling pools, the unfolding of God's plan starts on the mountaintop. From there the view of life is breathtaking and sobering. Our vision of God and of His plan for us moves our hearts—His design is so pure, so right, so uncluttered, and it makes sense! Having seen the beauty of the vision, we now have to go forward and *do* God's will. So we take a deep breath and brace ourselves. But how do we get started? Where do we begin? The woman who wrote this poem after coming to the peak where you and I now stand may express what you're feeling.

> So much material,
> So much to learn,
> So much to change,
> An overwhelming concern.

"Something is better than nothing,"
We are told.
And, again, wisdom and understanding
Are better than gold.

Where do I begin? I'm not even thin!
I move one step forward—two back,
I find my priorities all out of whack.
I *want* to be on the right track.

Pray for me, I need it so,
For I've got a long way to go.
Many things are obvious today,
The answer to this dilemma—PRAY![1]

If these words could be yours, take heart! We haven't yet come to the end. God has more guidelines for *how* to live out His will. Furthermore, God makes His will known as we read His Word, pray, and seek counsel. And He always enables us to do His will. God's grace is always sufficient to the task (2 Corinthians 12:9-10)! In fact, He has already given you everything you need to live your life in full godliness (2 Peter 1:3), and you can do all things—you can be a woman after His heart—through the strength of Jesus (Philippians 4:13). Take heart as we look at some how-to's.

A Word About Priorities

Because our lives are complex and demanding, we need a plan if we are to live by God's priorities and obey His call to us. God's order for priorities makes the day-to-day, moment-by-moment decisions easier and simpler. I can tell you wholeheartedly that the life-management system presented in this book works. It has brought order to my cluttered life and enabled me to see more clearly when the storms of life start to rage. God's unchangeable Word has given me sure guidance when the tyranny of the urgent beats on my door, trying to shove aside the very few *really* important tasks in my life—my grand duties and my chief works of:

- Loving God and following after Him with a whole heart,
- Loving, helping, and serving my husband,
- Loving and teaching my two daughters and their families,
- Loving and caring for my home in order to provide a quality life for my family,
- Developing myself so that I have something to give to others, and
- Loving and serving God's people.

Practicing these priorities calls us to wear many hats, and we must wear all of them—but we can only wear one at a time! Knowing what your priorities are—and choosing to wear the right hat at the right time—keeps you fully focused on the most important thing at hand at any given minute.

Remember, too, that these priorities are offered to you to help you make decisions about how to spend your time and energy. They are offered not as rigid guidelines, but to help you gain greater control over your life. This list of priorities and the discussion of them is meant to give you knowledge, skills, and motivation as you follow after God. So as you strive to live according to God's priorities, don't forget the principle of flexibility. Just as Jesus stopped and ministered to the bleeding woman on His way to raise Jairus' dead daughter (Luke 8:41-56), we need to be flexible, evaluating along the way—with each new event, crisis, or person—what the *real* priority is for that moment.

A Word About Choices

You've heard me say it many times, and here I go again! "The choices we make are key to the priorities we practice." From the first pages of this book, we've been trying to choose good over evil, better over good, and best over better. The importance of such choices cannot be overestimated or overemphasized. As we've all heard, if you want to know what you'll be like in the future, just look at the choices you are making today. As now, so then! It's something of a riddle.

> *Our choices, which reflect our priorities, will help us fulfill God's design for our lives.*

And so are these two thoughts: "What you are today (based on the choices you're making) is what you are becoming" and "You are today what you have been becoming (based on the choices you've already made)." Our choices, which reflect our priorities, will help us fulfill God's design for our lives. Getting everything done—or deciding what doesn't need to be done—is a matter of choice. Whether you are dealing with the next five minutes, the next hour, tomorrow, or forever, the choices you make make all the difference in the world!

A Word About Others

Have you noticed that we haven't yet gotten to some areas of life? I haven't mentioned parents, brothers, sisters, or extended family. And we haven't discussed jobs or careers, friends, neighbors, hobbies, pastimes, social life, or a myriad of other ingredients that make up your full and unique life. All these elements need to

be addressed and managed as we live a life that pleases God—
and all of them are to be enjoyed!
As the Bible says, "God...gives
us richly all things to enjoy"
(1 Timothy 6:17).

To adequately discuss the
long list of other people and
other ventures God has put into
your life would require another

> *God will reveal your priorities when you pray, search the Scriptures, and seek wise counsel.*

book. So for now, simply add those "other" categories to the end
of the list of the six priorities you've just looked at because those
six don't change. Each of these six aspects, these six roles we play,
is specifically addressed in the Bible. We've been looking at *God's*
plan, *God's* priorities, *God's* assignments. Our life situation may
change, but God's Word never changes. As the psalmist proclaims,
"The counsel of the LORD stands forever, the plans of His heart
to all generations" (Psalm 33:11)!

So I will leave it to you to prioritize the remaining areas of
your life. God will reveal the order to you when you pray, search
the Scriptures, and seek wise counsel. He will show you how to
be a woman after His heart in every detail of your life!

A Word About Waiting

It's impossible to read the book of Proverbs and not get the
message that *wisdom waits*. As a general principle for practicing
your priorities, know that it is safer to wait and do nothing than
to rush in and do the wrong thing. One of the many proverbs
that expresses this biblical truth says, "He sins who hastens with
his feet" (Proverbs 19:2).

Let me share how we applied this *wisdom waits* principle in
our home one hot summer day. The phone rang, and the call was

for my daughter Katherine from a friend I had neither met nor ever heard of. This teenage girl was inviting my daughter to go to the beach right away. Her message was, "We're leaving right now, and we'll pick you up in 15 minutes!"

Well, Katherine didn't go to the beach that day. Why? First of all, our day was already planned ("Plan A is always best" is one of my mottoes), and it didn't include her going to the beach. Also, Jim and I had not met this group of friends (Who was driving? Would boys be going?). This plan was definitely something we could say no to. And we could—and did—wait for a planned beach outing later on.

A friend of mine also had an opportunity to wait. Her mother-in-law was demanding a written letter of apology regarding a very difficult situation—and she wanted it *right now! It had to go out in today's mail so she could have it tomorrow or else!* My friend sent the letter—a week later. Why? Because she wanted to pray, have her heart right, share with her husband, seek counsel, and then have someone read the letter to help her word it so that it would truly accomplish God's purposes, which were indeed better served by waiting.

I myself had an opportunity to practice the *wisdom waits* principle when a breathless salesman called. "I'm calling from right around the corner," he said. "We're in your neighborhood today— and today only. This is the chance of a lifetime. We can clean all your carpets *right now* for only xxx dollars, *but it has to be right now!*" I didn't take him up on this deal. Why? Because, again, I'd already made plans for the day and they didn't include moving all our furniture and having all the carpets cleaned. They didn't include that kind of chaos. (We like to plan our chaos!) Also, I hadn't discussed having the carpets cleaned with my husband. Although it sounded like a bargain price to me, I'm not so sure

Jim would have thought that was the *best* use of that amount of money "*right now!*" Good, maybe, but best? Not so sure.

As that carpet cleaning offer illustrates, the telephone gives us a chance to practice the *wisdom waits* principle. It's always ringing, demanding our attention and presenting opportunities to get off our Plan A track. But you and I don't have to give those opportunities attention *right now!* Instead, we simply have to decide who's in control. Choosing to wait rather than acting impulsively is one way to gain or stay in control. A quote I've written in my prayer notebook reminds me that "very few things in life call for an instantaneous decision on your part….Keep your cool…. Make delay your first strategy for avoiding [chaos and crisis]…. A good rule of thumb to remember is that most things seem more important in the present than they actually are."[2] Wisdom waits. Will you?

Some Women Who Adjusted Their Priorities

One evening as I was reading (my "I'm going to read for just five minutes" time), I was struck by an account of a woman who seriously wanted to be God's kind of woman. Her name was Irene, and she was a Bible teacher much in demand. Her husband, Mike, however, was a nominal Christian who went to church but didn't get any more involved than that. Irene's priority list looked like this:

- God
- Teaching women's Bible studies
- Family

One day the Lord spoke to Irene through a verse in Ephesians: "Wives be subject—be submissive and adapt yourselves—to your own husband as (a service) to the Lord" (5:22).[3] When she saw this familiar verse in a different translation, Irene realized that serving her husband was a ministry, a service to the Lord. She began to seriously evaluate her life and her priorities.

Did she really love Mike? Did she put him first? She was everything to the Christian community she served, but not everything to Mike.

Irene dropped her outside activities and began to spend more time with Mike. When the church asked her to teach, she declined. When a friend asked her to lead a home Bible study, she refused. She stayed home with Mike. She watched TV with him, jogged with him, played cribbage, and made love to him. Irene dropped out of the picture as far as a visible Christian ministry was concerned. It was painful.

The subsequent two years were like "walking in a dark valley." Mike continued as a so-so Christian. Then in the middle of the third year, something stirred in Mike. He began to lead devotions and to do some teaching. His commitment to Christ solidified, and God began to develop him into a Christian leader. Irene realized that if she had remained in the limelight, Mike would have been too threatened to venture out. Today, at Mike's insistence, they teach together a class for couples. They have new priorities:

- God
- Each other
- Teaching Bible studies[4]

Irene took the significant step and reordered her priorities. Do you need to do the same? If so, please do it!

In another true story, a woman named Pat told of her ministry to inner-city kids. After a planning session for a theatrical production aimed at keeping the kids off the streets that summer, Pat dashed home at noon to see how her kids were doing.

As she arrived at the house, a police car pulled up behind her. Sitting in the backseat were her eight- and nine-year-old sons— frightened to death. While she was gone, the two boys had taken some matches from her kitchen and gone to a vacant lot to light firecrackers. The lot had caught fire, and the boys were appre- hended by the neighbors.

It suddenly became obvious to Pat which kids she should be trying to keep off the streets that summer. She called the inner- city office and resigned![5]

Pat reordered her priorities. Again, do you need to do the same? And again, if so, please do it now!

Heart Response

It sure is easy for priorities to get "out of whack," as my poet friend said! And making the choices to get back on track can sure be tough. But Irene and Pat are like you and me—wanting to do all God's will— and therefore willing to make the right choices even though they're the hard choices.

Is God speaking to you right now about how you are living your life? Is time with Him the first thing you seek each new day? David cried out to God in the wilderness:

> O God, You are my God;
> Early will I seek You;
> My soul thirsts for You;
> My flesh longs for You
> In a dry and thirsty land
> Where there is no water
> (Psalm 63:1).

Without a regular time with God, your Ultimate Priority, your life will be a dry and barren wilderness, and everything and everyone in it—including you—will suffer.

Continue now to move through the list of our priorities and evaluate how you're doing. Are you neglecting any of your priority people—your husband or your children? Is your home blossoming into a haven of rest, refreshment, beauty, and order for you and your loved ones? Are you using the firstfruits of your free time to be filled spiritually so that you can serve God and His people? And, finally, when you are with other people, are they refreshed by you, receiving out of the overflowing refreshment you find in the Lord? Put simply, are you seeking first things first—every day?

22

Following After God's Heart

My soul follows close behind You.
PSALM 63:8

If you and I are meeting for the first time in this book, you haven't yet visited my friend Judy's garden. In *Loving God with All Your Mind*,[1] I described the planning and planting Judy did. Now, these years later, I wish you could see her lovely and serene country garden. Judy has added much for her visitors to ooh and aah over. One of those additions is the arbor that her white iceberg roses have claimed as their own.

Whenever I stand on Judy's porch, my eye travels first to that sweet arbor, a quaint reminder of times gone by. The urge to stroll down the pressed gravel path that passes through its magical opening is irresistible. A delight to the senses, this gracious rose arbor provides gentle fragrance, cool shade, and refreshing beauty—and I'm never alone as I approach. Birds, butterflies, and

> *When you and I take seriously our assignments from God, He blesses our obedience, and the resulting growth is astounding.*

the neighbor's cat are also drawn there. All creatures—great and small—love Judy's rose arbor.

Needless to say, something this lovely is certainly no accident, and it didn't happen instantaneously. Much time and attention went into creating this lovely garden retreat, and the time and effort continue. Judy works hard tending her arbor, first faithfully feeding and tilling and watering the ground in the cool, early-morning stillness. Then, retrieving her sharpened shears from the storage shed, Judy begins the painstaking routine of cutting away unruly growth, pruning off unnecessary shoots, and removing dead blossoms. Performing this surgery—removing anything that would hinder the formation and development of her roses—is a crucial task. The meticulous training still remains to be done, and Judy does this by tacking down and wiring her roses, interweaving the loose branches and blooms, carefully directing and redirecting their growth. People enjoy a place of great beauty because of Judy's labor of love.

And, dear friend and follower after God's heart, people enjoy the beauty in our lives, our families, and our homes when we work in the same diligent and deliberate way Judy does. When you and I take seriously our assignments from God, He blesses our obedience, and the resulting growth is astounding. Oh, there are pleasant tasks and bright moments, but there is also plain old hard work—work that may be unexciting but gives birth to God's blessings.

As we end this book committed to following hard and close after God (as David did in Psalm 63:8) and doing His will (Acts

13:22), let's consider what we can do to nurture, prune, and train our hearts so that we can enjoy the lovely fruit God intends His people to know when they honor Him. What can we do to place ourselves before God so that we can know His beauty and serenity in our hearts and under our roofs?

Plan Your Day

Making God's plan for our lives a reality calls for planning on our part. The first challenge we face is gaining control of one day—today. We must tackle the day at hand, and—as I mentioned before—I find it helpful to consider each day's agenda at least twice.

First, the night before, when you climb into your wonderful, welcoming bed, take your planner with you (or a 3" x 5" card, or a "to do" list, or a legal pad—whatever). As you sit there relaxing, list in chronological order the concrete events of the next day—any appointments, meetings, or classes, the carpool, school and work schedules, and breakfast, lunch, and dinner. Whisper a prayer to God asking Him to guide and bless the next day— His day—and then turn off the light. You'll find that these few minutes can reduce the number of surprises in the morning— surprises like, "Oops, I forgot you needed a lunch!" "Now where is that dry cleaning?" "I can't believe I didn't cancel that dental appointment!" and "Oh no, it's trash day, and I forgot again!"

In the morning, welcome the day with the psalmist's words of praise—"This is the day the LORD has made; we will rejoice and be glad in it" (Psalm 118:24). Then take out a sheet of paper and get ready to create a plan for practicing God's priorities throughout the day. (I use an 8½" x 11" sheet of paper folded in half lengthwise.) Begin by praying.

Pray Over Your Plans and Priorities

What exactly should you pray about? Let me share some ideas by describing how I create a plan for practicing God's priorities.

God—First I write the word "God" on one side of my folded paper, and pray, "Lord, what can I do today to live out the fact that You are the Ultimate Priority of my life?"

As I pray, God usually leads me to list certain actions like pray, read His Word, memorize Scripture, walk with Him, be aware that He is present with me minute by minute. I write it all down.

Husband—Next I write the word "Jim." Again I go to the Lord for help, asking, "God, what can I do today to let Jim know he is my most important human priority?" (And if you're not married, move on down the list.)

At that point, for instance, God reminds me that I can choose to be "up" when Jim arrives home at the end of the day and to stay "up" throughout the evening. I can choose to be physically available to him. I can make plans for a special date night on Friday when the children are busy with their activities. And of course I can sew on that button!

Children—Now it's time to pray, "Lord, what can I do today for Katherine and Courtney to let them know that, after Jim, they are more important than all the other people in my life? What can I do to communicate to each one individually how special she is to me? How can I show each of them my love?" (Again, if you don't have children, move on down the list.)

Many times the answers to this question are "sweet speech," "kindness," "a servant spirit," and "no nagging." Just write down the answers and ideas. For instance, when my girls were toddlers, I scheduled specific times during each day to set aside all other activities and have a special time of playing or reading with them.

Other ideas that came to me as I prayed about my girls included, as they grew older, selecting a special card for each of them and writing a love note, or picking up some fresh bagels as I came home from Bible study, or preparing a favorite snack for them after school, or surprising them by picking them up after school for a cola instead of having them come home in the carpool.

Now that my girls are married, I make plans to communicate daily with each through email and to send them good books as little surprise gifts to help them build their own homes and encourage them in their personal growth and interests. Truly, the loving and praying and planning never cease. And then there are the grandchildren! Well, you get the picture.

Home—Everyone lives somewhere, including you, married or not. So land here and start praying because this one's for everyone. As I shared earlier, praying about homemaking lifts it out of the physical realm and transports it into the spiritual. So I pray, "Lord, what can I do today regarding my home? What can I do today to make our home a little bit of heaven, our own home sweet home?"

Something like "be faithful in daily cleaning tasks" will appear on my home list. "Finish fully" appears almost daily because it's a character quality and discipline I'm working on right now—especially in the evenings after dinner when I'm tired. I also write down special projects like "pull out dead summer flowers to make way for fresh autumn ones" and "research a remodel."

Self—I lay my life before God and pray, "Lord, what can I do today to grow spiritually? In what specific ways can I prepare for future ministry?"

Always the word *read* appears. "Exercise" and "food selection" show up often. Completing a Bible lesson, typing out quotations from books I've read, and getting to bed on time are other items. This is truly and by necessity a diverse list that suggests the wide-ranging activities and interests of life.

Ministry—"And, Lord," I continue praying, "what can I do today to serve and minister to Your people?" This is always the longest list as I write down people to call, friends and missionaries to write, lessons to plan, organizing, researching, writing, purchasing name tags, preparing food for church events or the ill, visiting the hospital. Opportunities for ministry are always all around us!

Because this list is so long, I go one step further. I ask God to help me prioritize it by praying, "God, if I could only do one of these labors of love today, which one would You want it to be? And if I could do two?"

Other activities—As I've continually said, this book focuses on our top priorities, those God-given assignments found in His Word. But I know (and certainly God does too) there are other facets to life. That's why I think of living out our priorities as being somewhat like an oil painting. The artist includes the elements of a painting—background, composition, subjects, style. The Impressionists, however, discovered that dotting an entire completed canvas with spots of another color added sparkle to the picture.

The same is true of our lives. We must follow all the rules and guidelines—as set forth by God in the Bible—so that our lives will contain all the elements necessary for beauty. But God, "who gives us richly all things to enjoy" (1 Timothy 6:17), blesses us with dots of color—with people, events, interests, desires, personalities, and challenges that add a unique sparkle.

In this category, then, I list shopping for Christmas, browsing in a library or bookstore, getting together with a friend, planning another trip to visit one of my daughters, replacing a pair of shoes. Again, this list goes on and on—its items are important, but not urgent.

Schedule Your Plans and Priorities

Now I have my list, and I can carry this handy piece of paper around all day, or put it on the refrigerator door, or lay it on the kitchen counter, or tape it onto my computer monitor. But items on the list only represent dreams and desires and convictions until we put them into practice. And scheduling helps us do just that. So at this point I put the other side of my paper to use. It becomes my schedule for practicing my priorities for the day. This is Round 2 in praying over and planning my day—a day I desire to live after God's heart.

I begin praying again, "Okay, God, *when* will I have my devotions? *When* will I meet with You in our special place?" I then write "devotions" in a specific time slot on my schedule. "And *when* will I sew on that button for Jim...and plan our Friday date?" I jot these down for precise times as well. "And *when* will I get those blueberry bagels for my blueberry girl?...Do those daily good housekeeping chores?...Read and exercise—even for five

> *If you follow these steps of planning, praying, and scheduling, you soon discover how comforting it is to get up from your time of prayer with a clear plan for your day.*

minutes!" I ask the Lord when to do all those things He and I both want done, and I write them all into my schedule for certain times during the day.

When my time of prayer and scheduling is over, I hold in my hand a master plan for the day—a plan that reflects my priorities, a plan that enables me to be the woman after God's own heart that I desire to be. Wisdom always has a plan (Proverbs 21:5).

If you follow these steps of planning, praying, and scheduling, you'll soon discover how comforting it is to get up from your time of prayer with a clear plan for your day. That plan is most effective when it comes as a result of much care and prayer—when it comes as a result of committing your day and its activities to God for His glory, when it comes from seeking God for guidance on the good, the better, and the best. Having made this kind of commitment and having done this seeking, determine to stick to your plan—God's plan.

Practice Your Priorities

Each day presents many opportunities and challenges to practice our priorities. One way to simplify your moment-by-moment decision-making might be to assign your priorities these numbers:

#1 — God

#2 — Your husband

#3 — Your children

#4 — Your home

#5 — Your spiritual growth

#6 — Your ministry activities

#7 — Other activities

Let me show you how this works.

- Your children (#3) have just arrived home from school, and you're praying and snacking and talking together about the day. The phone rings. It's not your husband (#2), which means it is either a ministry (#6), a friend (#7), or a salesperson. The decision is simple. You don't leave the #3 priority to tend to the #6 or #7 (or even lower) priority. Be sweet and be kind…but be firm and be brief. Make arrangements for a call back. Quickly ask the salesperson to remove your name and number from his or her call list. Don't lose this important time with your children!

- Your neighbor (#6—a ministry) knocks on the door and interrupts your time with your children (#3). What are you going to do? Again, I learned to be sweet and be kind… but be firm and be brief. Reschedule a visit for a time when the children are settled or busy with homework. Edith Schaeffer suggests you say something like this:

  > "I will see you later; right now I am having a half hour (or an hour) with Naomi." You should use the name of the [child]. When you say, "I am talking to Debby [your child]," you are stating to yourself as well as to the person, "This is a human being I have an important appointment with." Your child is a person…and children need to grow up knowing they are important to you, that their lives are valuable to you.[2]

- Your husband (#2) is home and the house is quiet as you share a few rare minutes together—and the phone rings. It's a woman needing counsel (#6), a friend who wants to chat (#7), or another salesman. The decision is straightforward, and you know it already. Be sweet and be kind… but be firm and be brief. Reschedule the visit for a time your husband (#2) is not at home.

These actions may sound harsh and heartless—like Judy cutting and training her roses on her arbor—but making these choices to live your priorities enables God to make your life a work of beauty. It's hard to make these choices and, yes, it can hurt, but they are necessary if our lives are to be what you and I—and God—desire them to be.

But take note. This planning—as important as it is—goes out the window in a true emergency. When Jim's mother was hospitalized, for instance, *all* activity ceased as Katherine and her husband, Paul, and I came alongside her. You can definitely regard a true need like this as God's new plan for your day…or three days. But our goal is to be discreet (Titus 2:5)—meaning women who are thinking things through and showing good judgment.

A woman of discretion thinks through her choices and the messages they deliver to her husband, her children, her neighbor. A woman of discretion thinks a situation through and considers all possible consequences, both good and bad. She weighs everything and—after some time spent praying, waiting on God, seeking His wisdom, and getting godly counsel—makes the right decision. You and I can do the same as we follow after God's heart!

Acquire God's Perspective on Your Day

As I prayerfully prioritize the activities of my day, God grants me a glimpse of His will for all the days of my life and that day in particular. This prioritizing also gives me a passion for what I am trying to achieve with my life efforts.

That passion has also been fueled by the following comments I first heard at a women's retreat when I was a young wife, the mom of two preschoolers, and about to enter the "Age 31" group (see below). Since the day I first heard these statements, they have motivated me to follow after God's plan for my life with all my heart, soul, mind, and strength. I want to pass these women's statements on to you in hopes that they will help fuel your passion and vision for God and His calling to you. But first let me set the stage.

A reporter interviewed four women and asked each of them what she thought about "the golden years," that period in life "after middle age traditionally characterized by wisdom, contentment, and useful leisure." Hear their thoughts—and fears.

Age 31: "Golden years? I have so much to do before then that I doubt I'll ever have them. I have to help my husband succeed. I want to raise our children decently to get them ready for a very tough world. And, of course, I want time for me, to find myself, to be my own person."

Age 44: "Only 20 years to go! I just hope we make it. If we can just get the kids through college and on their own, if we can just keep my husband's blood pressure under control and see me sanely through menopause....I'm just hoping we get there."

Age 53: "Doubtful. Sometimes I think our golden years will never come. My parents are still alive and need constant attention. Our daughter was divorced last year and lives with us again. Of course, she had a baby. And of course my husband and I feel responsible both for her and our grandson."

Age 63: "We're supposed to be on the brink, aren't we? Well, we're not. I'll be frank. We thought we were saving enough to live comfortably ever after, but we haven't. Inflation has eaten it up. Now my husband talks about deferring his retirement. If he does, so will I. We're keeping a house much too big for us. We're both unhappy about the way things have turned out."

Sobering comments, aren't they? As you and I stand looking down the corridor of time, life can appear so hopeless, so pointless, so futile. But now for God's vision, a godly perspective! It comes from a dear friend to whom I sent a copy of what you've just read. Here's her inspiring response:

Oh, Elizabeth—to treat each day as if it and it *alone* was our "golden day"—then what a beautiful string of golden days becoming golden years we would have to give back again to our Lord!

Imagine being a woman who treats each day as if it and it alone is her golden day! Now *that's* a woman after God's own heart. When I thought about this, I said, "That's it! Treating each day as if it and it alone is our golden day is the *how* of practicing priorities, and it's also the *why*—the motivation and the perspective we need—for practicing them."

Practice, Practice, Practice

That's what I want for you and me. I want us to approach each day as our golden day! To switch metaphors, I want your life and mine to be like a string of pearls, strung with day after day of precious days.

If you desire a good life, focus on having one good day, one quality day—today. After all, as someone has observed, "Every day is a little life, and our whole

> *Every day is God's gift of a fresh, unspoiled opportunity to live according to His priorities.*

life is but a single day repeated." So keep that focus on having a good day today and, at day's end, slip that single pearl onto your strand. The pearls on your strand will add up to a good life!

But what if yours was a day of failures? A day of merely trying to survive? A day of taking shortcuts? A day of neglecting things you wanted to focus on? We all have those days. But thanks be to God who enables us to forget the day that is done, to reach forward the next morning, and to press on toward the goal—the pearl—again and again and again (Philippians 3:13-14)! In His power and by His grace, we keep following after God's heart—no matter what.

After all, every morning He gives you a fresh new day, His gift of a fresh, unspoiled opportunity to live according to His priorities. Furthermore, by exercising the privilege of confession and because of Jesus' forgiveness, you have a clean start with the dawn. God's mercies are new every morning, and His faithfulness is great (Lamentations 3:22-23)! So every morning remember that your goal is simple. You want to have just one good day of living your priorities. Then keep focused on following God's plan for your life for just this one day. For just one day, try putting first things first.

When such a focused day is done, you'll probably be tired as you drop into bed. I know I am! But you'll also know an unmatchable peace in your heart. A peace that comes from resting in the Lord and doing things His way. A peace that comes from knowing that because you lived out God's priorities for you, all is well under your roof.

Why this peace? Because you sought the Lord and followed close after Him the whole day! The people in your life were loved and served out of the overflow of your full heart. Your home was cared for—and God's beauty and order reigned there in the refuge you created. You took care of yourself and grew as God stretched you in preparation for serving Him. And you did serve—anyone and everyone who crossed your path. You reached out, looked out, gave out, and lived out God's priorities for a woman after His heart.

And then there were the other things—perhaps your dear parents, needy souls at your place of employment, special friends, time with a hurting neighbor, crafts to be made for giving away at the appropriate time. On and on your golden day went as you looked to God for His guidance, wisdom, and strength, as you loved Him by faithfully obeying Him, and as you leaned on Him during the challenges and trials of the day.

It was indeed a full day—but oh, what a rich one. And yes, your body is tired—but oh, what

> *So at the end of your day, your heart is satisfied and content. You have done the giving, the living, the following, and the loving. In return, God satisfied your longing heart and filled your hungry soul with his goodness.*

a satisfying tiredness. And, yes, it may not look like you've done much (there's no big splash, no headline news, nothing to tell anyone about)—but oh, the depth of the fullness you sense in your heart as God whispers to you, "Well done!"

As you finally stretch out in bed, wearily pull up the covers, and sink your head into the waiting pillow, you can know you have slipped another pearl onto your strand. This costly pearl is the most magnificent prize awaiting a woman after God's own heart. The reward for living life God's way is immeasurably, unspeakably, and indescribably wonderful. I'm struggling to find the words.

So at the end of your day, your heart is satisfied and content. You have done the giving, the living, the following, and the loving. In return, God satisfied your longing heart and filled your hungry soul with His goodness (Psalm 107:9). The peace you sense is the satisfaction that comes from gladly being spent in doing God's will, from being a woman after God's own heart—for just one day.

Now...let that one day—that one step—encourage you to string your *daily* pearls into a *lifetime* of living as a woman after God's own heart!

Part 4

In Praise
of God's Priorities

23

The Legacy of A Woman After God's Own Heart

For David,
after he had served his own generation
by the will of God, fell asleep.
ACTS 13:36

In the first few pages of this book I asked you to carefully consider David's usefulness to God as reported in Acts 13:22: "[God] raised up for them David as king, to whom also He gave testimony and said, 'I have found David the son of Jesse, a man after My own heart, who will do My will.'" Even with all of his faults, David had a heart for God—he desired to do God's will.

And now, dear heart sister, you and I have come full circle in our study of David's heart for God and our own full hearts. The apostle Paul's account of David's life began with an evaluation of

David's heart, and it ends with the results of his heart's commitment—David "served his own generation by the will of God" (Acts 13:36).

David's last will and testament is that his life had an impact. He served his own generation by the will of God. Why...and how? Because David chose to submit his heart and service to God's will, not his own.

Ten Years Later...

It's been much more than ten years since I began teaching this material about becoming a woman after God's own heart. In this book...and when given the opportunity to speak on this topic... I have attempted to give you a glimpse into some of my own personal struggles as I desired and sought to become a woman after God's own heart, a woman who desires to do God's will. It certainly hasn't been easy. Sometimes I take one step forward and then quickly fall two steps back.

But energized and encouraged by the grace of God and propelled by my heart's desire to love God through obedience, I continued to move forward, be it ever so slowly. You see, I wanted (and still want) to serve my "own generation"—especially my husband and children, and now seven new members of a new generation! I wanted (and still want) my family to have the best I could be and the best I could give. And I wanted (and still do) to do it God's way—by following God's will, God's plan.

In the decade since I initially wrote this book, I have had great positive feedback from women like you who have read this book, or heard me speak on some portion of it, or participated in one of the "A Woman After God's Own Heart" video classes. So now I want to take these final few pages and share my own reflections on the past decade and also some reflections from others.

Reflections from a Woman After God's Own Heart

During these past ten-plus years, my life has changed dramatically. Our daughters met and married their wonderful husbands, had their babies, and their families have moved to the far ends of the United States (we live on the West Coast and they now live on the East Coast). On the other end of our lives, I lost both of my parents, and Jim lost his mother, his last living parent. Jim retired from The Master's Seminary to write and speak full time (which means he and I are not only busier than ever, but we are together 24/7!).

Believe me, nothing has slowed down. No, we moved quickly from the fast lane right into warp speed! We now have our daughters and sons-in-law and seven grandchildren, to whom we are fiercely committed. Plus both of us are writing daily as well as speaking on a regular basis while still growing in the Lord.

But even with all of these changes—and through them all—the priorities I write about in this book have been my guiding beacon. And, praise God, He has sustained me and enabled me to stay on target—to love Him first and passionately, to be the best wife and mom and grandmom I can possibly be, to continue growing in my knowledge of God, and to serve Him and His people. How can this be? Certainly it is to the praise of God's all-sufficient grace. And also partly it is because I have attempted with my whole heart (I hope and pray!) to practice and order my life by the priorities I talk about in this book—priorities I learned from God's manual for all of life, the Bible. I desired (and still do) and prayed (and still do) to have a heart that obeyed each and every time a new or difficult challenge came along. And, praise God again, I have witnessed and experienced His blessings!

How I would love to say I passed each test with flying colors!

But sadly, at times I slipped up. (I have my share of sad or bad memories.) But God, who knows all, knew my heart. He knew that I dearly wanted to follow Him, and His grace was definitely substantial, adequate, and enough—totally sufficient!

As I have reviewed this book and made the important updates and revisions, I have to say that these principles truly worked in my life...and still do. Through the decades and seasons of Christian growth and marriage and family and change, I have repeatedly revisited the priorities I wrote about in this book. And I have to report, I am convinced more than ever, that if I, or you, will follow God's priorities for us, our lives, as well as the lives of our loved ones and the lives of others who watch us or who are mentored by us, will be forever positively impacted. And on top of that, miracles of miracles, God will be honored and glorified (Titus 2:5)!

Reflections from Other Women After God's Own Heart

As Jim and I travel, I have the opportunity to meet and interact with thousands of wonderful Christian women. I also hear from thousands of others through mail and email. I am not one who saves letters and email, although I do try to answer each woman. (And during the process of revisiting this book, I wished I had saved both the communication from women and my responses to them!) What I wish to do here is share with you a composite of what so many have written. Perhaps you'll find your own heart response here.

Wives of many years—This band of married-for-many-years women has discovered and testified that "it's never too late to begin practicing your priorities." It's never too late to begin to follow God's commands and live out your assignment from God as a loving and supportive wife.

Let me give you one little story…

> At a woman's conference, I was sitting at the auto-graphing table and a young woman and her mother came through the line to have me sign their well-worn copies of *A Woman After God's Own Heart*®. The daughter playfully poked her mom with her elbow and said, "Go ahead, Mom. Tell Mrs. George what happened." And so Mom shared!
>
> It seems that after the daughter and her mom began reading this book, the mom (married, lo, almost 40 years!) began practicing some of the principles I lay out in the "husband section." Her husband was in the process of retiring and took advantage of an exit physical exam provided by his company. Well, several weeks after the exam he asked his wife, "Honey, am I dying?"
>
> Stunned, she asked, "Why, no, not that I know of? Why? Why would you ask such a thing?"
>
> Her husband explained, "Well, I haven't heard anything from the doctor, and I thought maybe he had called you with bad news—to let you know I was dying—and that's why you have been so nice to me."

One absolutely marvelous thing about this true story is that this wife (even at "retirement" age!) was beginning to practice what she was reading and learning from God's Word—and her husband had noticed!

Another good thing is that it clearly demonstrates that it's never too late in your marriage to begin to practice God's priorities as a wife, even if you have been married 40 years.

Newlyweds—There's no way to count the number of times I've heard this comment: "I wish I'd had this book 20 years ago when I first got married!" This is one of the most often verbalized reflections of those who are married and have read this book.

And I am always quick to add, "Me too!"

Many newlyweds have also been spared from learning about marriage the hard way or later in their marriages because some caring women gave them this book as bridal shower gifts or wedding gifts. Furthermore, young marrieds have learned and responded to these biblical principles because some wise women gave them copies and used them as mentoring or counseling tools. You know newlyweds…they have very little money. And these dear ones probably would not have bought the book on their own.

And too because stars were in their eyes and fantasies filled their hearts, these brides probably didn't have a clue as to what marriage is really all about. They had no hint as to their roles and responsibilities as Christian women, let alone as wives! But I praise God that they read the book, followed the biblical principles, and then communicated with me to share their excitement and appreciation for the information. How I applaud their tender hearts that were sensitive to God's ways!

Single gals—On many occasions I have had single women write or introduce themselves at a conference who commented that upon reading the book, they were struck by how little of it actually applied to wives and moms only. They were prepared to feel left out and overlooked. But because they went ahead and read the book, they were delighted to discover that of the six priorities addressed in this book, only two apply directly to wives and moms. Refreshingly, the remainder of the book applied to and addressed *all* Christian women. The book wrapped its arms around them and drew them in. There was plenty of meat for them to chew on.

If you are single, I want to say to you that even the chapters dealing with marriage and family can be tremendously powerful and helpful tools as you mentor or counsel or teach others. If your heart and ears are open, you'll have countless opportunities as you sense or hear the distress of other friends, co-workers, even strangers, who are married women and moms with problems. And all you have to do is open your mouth and share with them what the Bible says about their situations. You may even want to open your pocketbooks and bless them with their very own copies of these life-changing, marriage-saving, family-preserving principles.

And who knows, maybe something from one or both of these sections on marriage and family might be of help to you as you pursue a life of godly character.

Working wives—When I originally began teaching these principles, less than 50 percent of Christian women worked outside their homes. Now that figure is closer to 70 percent. What has been the reaction of these working wives and moms?

Well, it has been overwhelmingly positive! This group of woman has been greatly encouraged as they gain greater insights into their real and most meaningful assignments in life—those of wife, mom, and homemaker. Yes, they work at "outside" jobs, but they now understand God's priorities and are embracing them as their own. They may have jobs and do those jobs heartily unto the Lord. But each woman now has a better understanding of what her real job is—practicing her God-given priorities.

And no, it isn't easy. Yet these working wives now know and recognize that essentially they have two full-time jobs, the first and most important one at home with their families, and the other at the office, the store, the schoolroom, or the hospital.

Stay-at-home wives—The letters and comments have been overwhelmingly positive from the group of ladies who stay at home. They have written with words of appreciation for the help given in this book that enables them to prioritize their busy and active homes and families. They testify that before they read *A Woman After God's Own Heart®*, they were busy doing many things—too many things—and many of the wrong things. Yes, they were at home, but their priorities were all in the wrong place...or "all out of whack" as the poem in chapter 21 puts it! The principles from the Bible shared in this book helped them reorient to God's priorities and bear good fruit... and better fruit...and the best fruit.

Concerned women—As I said, my Jim retired from teaching and administrating and began writing. His first book project came as a result of the mountains of letters and numerous comments from many wives who were reading my book *A Woman After God's Own Heart®*. Because they were now understanding their priorities and reaping the blessings from practicing them, they wanted to know if there was anything for their husband about his priorities. Jim's first book was appropriately entitled *A Man After God's Own Heart.*[1]

Then came requests from concerned wives and moms for something just for their marriages (not only for themselves, but also for their husbands). And there were cries for help from moms for more on loving and raising their children…and for their husbands as dads. Next came specific inquiries—"Do you have anything for my teen daughter…or son…or for my little ones?" Due to the need and desire for help, a groundswell was created by women who want to be women and wives and moms who follow after God. In time, and by God's grace, both Jim and I have written books that address these requests for information. (See our book list at the back of this book.)

What a joy it is for Jim and me to go to our mailbox daily and learn how women and men and teens and little ones are beginning to understand and live out God's wisdom and plan as they read these additional books. Just think of the marriages and families and children who are benefiting as they seek to live out God's plan! They, by the will of God, are serving their own generation as they follow after God's own heart.

24

The Legacy of
Your Heart

Be diligent to present yourself approved to God,
a worker who does not need to be ashamed....
2 TIMOTHY 2:15

Reflection Time for You, a Woman After God's Own Heart

I hope you benefited from what I shared about other readers of this book in the last chapter. And now, having said all of that about those who have discovered God's design and begun to implement some or all of the principles we have talked about throughout this book, where might you start?

First of all, I am assuming you are responding positively to what I have written. At least (I hope and pray!) you didn't throw your book across the room when you hit any sensitive points. I am believing, since you made it to the end and to this final chapter, that you are ready to "go for it"…and have been doing so for 24 chapters! You are probably implementing many of the principles we have discussed so far. Well done! Please continue your journey to become a woman truly after God's own heart.

As the scripture at the beginning of the previous chapter bore witness, "David, after he had served his own generation by the will of God, fell asleep." Now, don't you desire to be a woman who serves her generation, whether that's the people at home—your husband, sons and daughters, grandsons and granddaughters… or parents or in-laws—or in your neighborhood or apartment building, or at church, or out in the workplace?

Here, dear friend and heart sister, are a few keys that have helped me in my desire to become—and keep on becoming—a woman after God's own heart. I pray they will encourage and help you as well.

Becoming a Woman After God's Own Heart

Key #1: Obey God's commands

I'm sure you agree that obedience to God and His commands is the primary key to the Christian life. As God told King Saul through the prophet Samuel, "To obey is better than sacrifice" (1 Samuel 15:22). You see, God doesn't want your outward obedience to be a ritual. Oh no, He wants your heart! He wants you to respond in obedience to His Word as He speaks directly to your situation. Your greatest impact will come as you "serve your generation by the will of God"—which means choosing to do things God's way, not your own way.

Obedience is not always easy. In fact, it's usually very difficult. Why? Because your (and my) human flesh wants to do things its way. There is a battle going on in your heart between doing what you should do and doing what you want to do.

How do you deal with this battle in your heart?

Key #2: Walk in the Spirit

You manage the battle in your heart by following this next key as you seek to "walk in the Spirit" (Galatians 5:16). When you "walk in the Spirit...you shall not fulfill the lust of the flesh." Looking to God for His help and obeying this one command will do away with the works of the flesh, which destroy lives, marriages, families, and homes (verses 19-21). As you ask for help from God and walk with Him according to His ways, you reap instead "the fruit of the Spirit," which is "love, joy, peace, longsuffering, kindness, goodness, faithfulness, gentleness, self-control" (verses 22-23). Imagine the heart, the life—and the marriage, family, and home!—where such fruit abounds.

My reading friend, you get started down this fruitful path by acknowledging to God that you want to follow Him. Go ahead and tell God if you don't quite understand how it's all going to work or work out. But also ask Him for the grace and strength to trust Him, to walk by faith. You'll notice a change right away in your walk!

Key #3: Pray regularly

I've already referred to prayer, but as you well know from reading this book, the role of prayer is so very important to fulfilling God's will for your life. It's vital! Prayer acknowledges your dependence on God. Prayer opens your heart to knowing and fulfilling God's will. Prayer gives you the assurance and confidence that, as you carry out God's priorities, He will give you the strength to see it through to the end. Dear one, if you want to serve your generation as a woman after God's own heart, then prayer must become an all-important part of your life.

Key #4: Adopt a long-range view

It took David a lifetime to fulfill God's will and serve his generation. And, beloved, it has taken me more than 20 years to come to the place in my life where I'm beginning to understand what it means to serve my generation. You've taken a good number of days or weeks to read and digest this book. Many of the concepts might have been foreign or difficult for you to understand and begin to implement. Please understand that something this important—as important as doing God's will and living out His priorities—will take a long time to complete. Indeed, it will take a lifetime. It's not something you can start and finish in a few days, weeks, months, or years. No, it is a long-range, life-long, wholehearted assignment from God. But be encouraged! This lifestyle is lived—and built—by following after God just one day at a time...and another day...and another day. So each day focus on the tasks and people in front of you.

Key #5: Accept your roles

This may seem somewhat similar to Key #4, except this key requires that you take on the task of being a woman after God's own heart in a personal way. It's one thing to have a goal, but it's quite another thing to actually accept the challenge, develop a strategy to press for the goal, make the sacrifices, pay the price to move forward, and blessing of blessings, to realize some part of it. This is where resolve and desire come in. Do you really believe God is asking you to serve your generation...and to serve according to His will? It seems so obvious, but until you accept your assignment as coming from God Himself, you will have difficulty taking it seriously. We simply cannot play around with taking such a high calling lightly. The lives and well-being of others are at stake...are at risk!

Never give up.

Key #6: Ask, "Who am I, and what is it I do?"

Each of God's women is at a different season in life. And for each, that season is also changing. I don't know where life finds you today. And I've shared a little about my present life challenges. But perhaps you are single...or married—with or without children who are younger or older, or somewhere in between. You may be older or younger in age. Whatever your (and my) age and stage, you must be constantly asking yourself, "Who am I?" Hopefully by now you will always answer this question with "I am a woman after God's own heart!"

And the second question you must constantly ask is, "What is it I do?" I'm sure you sense by now that the answer to this question will constantly change. And with each change, you make the necessary adjustments. As you daily seek with all your heart to follow God's laid-out plans and priorities for you, to walk by His Spirit, and to pray faithfully, He will help you make the choices that guide you into His path for each stage and age of your life. You will then forever be His woman, a woman after His very own heart.

Quiet Times Calendar

Jan.	Feb.	Mar.	Apr.	May	June
1	1	1	1	1	1
2	2	2	2	2	2
3	3	3	3	3	3
4	4	4	4	4	4
5	5	5	5	5	5
6	6	6	6	6	6
7	7	7	7	7	7
8	8	8	8	8	8
9	9	9	9	9	9
10	10	10	10	10	10
11	11	11	11	11	11
12	12	12	12	12	12
13	13	13	13	13	13
14	14	14	14	14	14
15	15	15	15	15	15
16	16	16	16	16	16
17	17	17	17	17	17
18	18	18	18	18	18
19	19	19	19	19	19
20	20	20	20	20	20
21	21	21	21	21	21
22	22	22	22	22	22
23	23	23	23	23	23
24	24	24	24	24	24
25	25	25	25	25	25
26	26	26	26	26	26
27	27	27	27	27	27
28	28	28	28	28	28
29	29	29	29	29	29
30		30	30	30	30
31		31		31	

Date Begun _____

July	Aug.	Sept.	Oct.	Nov.	Dec.
1	1	1	1	1	1
2	2	2	2	2	2
3	3	3	3	3	3
4	4	4	4	4	4
5	5	5	5	5	5
6	6	6	6	6	6
7	7	7	7	7	7
8	8	8	8	8	8
9	9	9	9	9	9
10	10	10	10	10	10
11	11	11	11	11	11
12	12	12	12	12	12
13	13	13	13	13	13
14	14	14	14	14	14
15	15	15	15	15	15
16	16	16	16	16	16
17	17	17	17	17	17
18	18	18	18	18	18
19	19	19	19	19	19
20	20	20	20	20	20
21	21	21	21	21	21
22	22	22	22	22	22
23	23	23	23	23	23
24	24	24	24	24	24
25	25	25	25	25	25
26	26	26	26	26	26
27	27	27	27	27	27
28	28	28	28	28	28
29	29	29	29	29	29
30	30	30	30	30	30
31	31		31		31

Notes

Dear Seeker

1. To order or learn more about the 10-session "A Woman After God's Own Heart Video Bible Study" taught by Elizabeth George, visit www.ElizabethGeorge.com or call 1-800-542-4611.

A Word of Welcome

1. Richard Foster, "And We Can Live by It: Discipline," *Decision Magazine,* September 1982, p. 11.
2. Ibid.

Chapter 1—A Heart Devoted to God

1. Ray and Anne Ortlund, *The Best Half of Life* (Glendale, CA: Regal Books, 1976), p. 88.
2. Carole Mayhall, *From the Heart of a Woman* (Colorado Springs: NavPress, 1976), pp. 10-11.
3. Oswald J. Smith, *The Man God Uses* (London: Marshall, Morgan & Scott, 1925), pp. 52-57.
4. Andrew Murray, on a bookmark.
5. Quoted in Ortlund and Ortlund, *The Best Half of Life,* pp. 24-25.
6. Betty Scott Stam, source unknown.

Chapter 2—A Heart Abiding in God's Word

1. Ray and Anne Ortlund, *The Best Half of Life* (Glendale, CA: Regal Books, 1976), p. 79.
2. C.A. Stoddards, source unknown.
3. Henry Drummond, *The Greatest Thing in the World* (Old Tappan, NJ: Fleming H. Revell Company, 1977), p. 42.
4. Jim Downing, *Meditation, The Bible Tells You How* (Colorado Springs: NavPress, 1976), pp. 15-16.
5. Robert D. Foster, *The Navigator* (Colorado Springs: NavPress, 1983), pp. 110-11.
6. Quoted in J.C. Pollock, *Hudson Taylor and Maria* (Grand Rapids, MI: Zondervan, 1975), p. 169.
7. Ibid., p. 169.
8. Anne Ortlund, *The Disciplines of the Beautiful Woman* (Waco, TX: Word, Inc., 1977), p. 103.
9. Mrs. Charles E. Cowman, *Streams in the Desert—Vol. 1* (Grand Rapids, MI: Zondervan, 1965), p. 330.
10. Cited in Foster, *The Navigator,* pp. 64-65.
11. Obituary of William Schuman, *Los Angeles Times,* February 17, 1992.

Chapter 3—A Heart Committed to Prayer

1. Corrie ten Boom, *Don't Wrestle, Just Nestle* (Old Tappan, NJ: Revell, 1978), p. 79.
2. Oswald Chambers, *Christian Disciplines* (Grand Rapids, MI: Discovery House Publishers, 1995), p. 117.
3. Clarion Classics, *The Prayers of Suzanna Wesley* (Grand Rapids, MI: Zondervan Publishing House, 1984), p. 51.
4. Ibid., p. 49.

5.   Ibid., p. 54.

6.   James Dobson, *What Wives Wish Their Husbands Knew About Women* (Wheaton, IL: Tyndale House Publishers, Inc., 1977), p. 22.

7.   Edith Schaeffer, *Common Sense Christian Living* (Nashville: Thomas Nelson Publishers, 1983), pp. 212-15.

8.   Ibid.

Chapter 4—A Heart That Obeys

1.   Curtis Vaughan, ed., *The Old Testament Books of Poetry from 26 Translations* (Grand Rapids, MI: Zondervan Bible Publishers, 1973), pp. 478-79.

2.   Ibid., p. 277.

Chapter 5—A Heart That Serves

1.   Charles F. Pfeiffer and Everett F. Harrison, eds., *The Wycliffe Bible Commentary* (Chicago: Moody Press, 1973), p. 5.

2.   Ray and Anne Ortlund, *The Best Half of Life* (Glendale, CA: Regal Books, 1976), p. 97.

3.   Julie Nixon Eisenhower, *Special People* (New York: Ballantine Books, 1977), p. 199.

4.   Quoted in Ibid., p. 80.

Chapter 6—A Heart That Follows

1.   *Webster's New Collegiate Dictionary* (Springfield, MA: G. & C. Merriam Co., Publishers, 1961), s.v. submission.

2.   Elisabeth Elliot, *The Shaping of a Christian Family* (Nashville: Thomas Nelson Publishers, 1992), p. 75.

3.   Sheldon Vanauken, *Under the Mercy* (San Francisco: Ignatius Press, 1985), pp. 194-95.

Chapter 7—A Heart That Loves—Part 1

1.   Gene Getz, *The Measure of a Woman* (Glendale, CA: Gospel Light Publications, 1977), pp. 75-76.

2.   Jill Briscoe and Judy Golz, *Space to Breathe, Room to Grow* (Wheaton, IL: Victor Books, 1985), pp. 184-87.

3.   Anne Ortlund, *Building a Great Marriage* (Old Tappan, NJ: Fleming H. Revell Company, 1984), p. 146.

4.   Howard and Charlotte Clinebell, quoted in ibid., p. 170.

5.   Charlie Shedd, *Talk to Me* (Old Tappan, NJ: Fleming H. Revell Company, 1976), pp. 65-66.

6.   Curtis Vaughan, ed., *The Old Testament Books of Poetry from 26 Translations* (Grand Rapids, MI: Zondervan Bible Publishers, 1973), p. 572.

Chapter 8—A Heart That Loves—Part 2

1.   Edith Schaeffer, *What Is a Family?* (Old Tappan, NJ: Fleming H. Revell Company, 1975), p. 87.

2.   Jack and Carole Mayhall, *Marriage Takes More Than Love* (Colorado Springs: NavPress, 1978), p. 154, quoting Kay K. Arvin, *One Plus One Equals One* (Nashville: Broadman Press, 1969), pp. 37-38.

3.   Anne Ortlund, *Building a Great Marriage* (Old Tappan, NJ: Fleming H. Revell Company, 1984), p. 157.

4.   Julie Nixon Eisenhower, *Special People* (New York: Ballantine Books, 1977), pp. 52-53.

5.   Betty Frist, *My Neighbors, The Billy Grahams* (Nashville: Broadman Press, 1983), p. 31.

6.   William MacDonald, *Enjoying the Proverbs* (Kansas City, KS: Walterick Publishers, 1982), p. 56.

Chapter 9—A Heart That Values Being a Mother

1.   Phil Whisenhunt, *Good News Broadcaster,* May 1971, p. 20.

2.   Stanley High, *Billy Graham* (New York: McGraw Hill, 1956), p. 28.

3. Quoted in High, *Billy Graham*, p. 126.
4. Carole C. Carlson, *Corrie ten Boom: Her Life, Her Faith* (Old Tappan, NJ: Fleming H. Revell Company, 1983), p. 33.
5. Elisabeth Elliot, *The Shaping of a Christian Family* (Nashville: Thomas Nelson Publishers, 1992), p. 58.
6. Mrs. Howard Taylor, *John and Betty Stam: A Story of Triumph*, rev. ed. (Chicago: Moody Press, 1982), p. 15.
7. Elliot, *Shaping of a Christian Family*, pp. 205-06.

Chapter 10—A Heart That Prays Faithfully
1. H.D.M. Spence and Joseph S. Exell, eds., *The Pulpit Commentary, Volume 9* (Grand Rapids, MI: Wm. B. Eerdmans Publishing Company, 1978), p. 595.
2. Charles Bridges, *A Modern Study in the Book of Proverbs*, rev. by George F. Santa (Milford, MI: Mott Media, 1978), p. 728.
3. Spence and Exell, eds., *Pulpit Commentary, Volume 9*, p. 607.
4. Stanley High, *Billy Graham* (New York: McGraw Hill, 1956), p. 71.
5. Linda Raney Wright, *Raising Children* (Wheaton, IL: Tyndale House Publishers, Inc., 1975), p. 50.
6. E. Schuyler English, *Ordained of the Lord* (Neptune, NJ: Loizeaux Brothers, 1976), p. 35.

Chapter 11—A Heart Overflowing with Motherly Affection—Part 1
1. Marvin R. Vincent, *Word Studies in the New Testament*, vol. IV (Grand Rapids, MI: Wm. B. Eerdmans Publishing Co., 1973), p. 341.
2. Dwight Spotts, "What Is Child Abuse?" in *Parents & Teenagers*, Jay Kesler, ed. (Wheaton, IL: Victor Books, 1984), p. 426.
3. Curtis Vaughan, ed., *The Old Testament Books of Poetry from 26 Translations* (Grand Rapids, MI: Zondervan Bible Publishers, 1973), p. 399.
4. Gary Smalley, *For Better or for Best* (Grand Rapids, MI: Zondervan Publishing House, 1988), p. 95.
5. Edith Schaeffer, *What Is a Family?* (Old Tappan, NJ: Fleming H. Revell Company, 1975).

Chapter 12—A Heart Overflowing with Motherly Affection—Part 2
1. Julie Nixon Eisenhower, *Special People* (New York: Ballantine Books, 1977), p. 69.
2. Linda Dillow, *Creative Counterpart* (Nashville: Thomas Nelson Publishers, 1977), p. 24.

Chapter 13—A Heart That Makes a House a Home
1. Catherine Marshall, *A Man Called Peter* (New York: McGraw-Hill, 1961), p. 65.
2. James Strong, *Strong's Exhaustive Concordance of the Bible* (Nashville: Abingdon Press, 1973), p. 22.
3. Robert Alden, *Proverbs* (Grand Rapids, MI: Baker Book House, 1983), p. 110.
4. Edith Schaeffer, *What Is a Family?* (Old Tappan, NJ: Fleming H. Revell Company, 1975).
5. Julie Nixon Eisenhower, *Special People* (New York: Ballantine Books, 1977), p. 209.
6. Jim Conway, *Men in Mid-Life Crisis* (Elgin, IL: David C. Cook Publishing Company, 1987), pp. 250-52.
7. Edith Schaeffer, *Tapestry* (Waco, TX: Word Books, 1981), p. 616.
8. Strong, *Strong's Exhaustive Concordance*, p. 34.
9. William J. Peterson, *Martin Luther Had a Wife* (Wheaton, IL: Tyndale House Publishers, Inc., 1983), p. 67.
10. Bonnie McCullough, *Los Angeles Times*, date unknown.

Chapter 14—A Heart That Watches Over the Home
1. Jo Berry, *The Happy Home Handbook* (Old Tappan, NJ: Fleming H. Revell Co., 1976).
2. James Strong, *Strong's Exhaustive Concordance of the Bible* (Nashville: Abingdon Press, 1973), p. 118.

3.   H.D.M. Spence and Joseph S. Exell, *Pulpit Commentary, Vol. 8* (Grand Rapids, MI: Wm. B. Eerdmans Publishing Company, 1978), p. 30.

4.   Derek Kidner, *Psalms 1–72* (Downers Grove, IL: InterVarsity Press, 1973), p. 58.

5.   William Peterson, *Martin Luther Had a Wife* (Wheaton, IL: Tyndale House Publishers, Inc., 1983), p. 81.

Chapter 15—A Heart That Creates Order from Chaos

1.   Curtis Vaughan, ed., *The New Testament from 26 Translations* (Grand Rapids, MI: Zondervan Publishing House, 1967), p. 981.

2.   James Strong, *Strong's Exhaustive Concordance of the Bible* (Nashville: Abingdon Press, 1973), p. 51.

3.   William Peterson, *Martin Luther Had a Wife* (Wheaton, IL: Tyndale House Publishers, Inc., 1983), p. 27.

4.   Alan Lakein, *How to Control Your Time and Your Life* (New York: Signet Books, 1974), p. 48.

Chapter 16—A Heart That Weaves a Tapestry of Beauty

1.   H.D.M. Spence and Joseph S. Exell, eds., *The Pulpit Commentary, Volume 21* (Grand Rapids, MI: Wm. B. Eerdmans Publishing Company, 1978), p. 36.

2.   James Strong, *Strong's Exhaustive Concordance of the Bible* (Nashville: Abingdon Press, 1973), p. 51.

3.   Donald Guthrie, *Tyndale New Testament Commentaries, The Pastoral Epistles* (Grand Rapids, MI: Wm. B. Eerdmans Publishing Company, 1976), p. 194.

4.   Robert Jamieson, A.R. Fausset, and David Brown, *Commentary on the Whole Bible* (Grand Rapids, MI: Zondervan Publishing House, 1973), p. 1387.

5.   Curtis Vaughan, ed., *The New Testament from 26 Translations* (Grand Rapids, MI: Zondervan Publishing House, 1967), p. 1017.

6.   Anne Ortlund, *Love Me with Tough Love* (Waco, TX: Word, Incorporated, 1979).

Chapter 17—A Heart Strengthened by Spiritual Growth

1.   Ted W. Engstrom, *The Pursuit of Excellence* (Grand Rapids, MI: Zondervan Publishing House, 1982), pp. 30-31.

2.   Anne Ortlund, *The Disciplines of the Beautiful Woman* (Waco, TX: Word, Incorporated, 1977), pp. 96, 98.

Chapter 18—A Heart Enriched by Joy in the Lord

1.   Check out Moody Correspondence School, 820 North LaSalle Street, Chicago, IL 60610, 1-800-621-7105.

2.   Jack and Carole Mayhall, *Marriage Takes More Than Love* (Colorado Springs: NavPress, 1978), p. 157.

3.   Betty Frist, *My Neighbors, The Billy Grahams* (Nashville: Broadman Press, 1983), p. 143.

4.   Michael LeBoeuf, *Working Smart* (New York: Warner Books, 1979), p. 182.

5.   Ted W. Engstrom, *The Pursuit of Excellence* (Grand Rapids, MI: Zondervan Publishing House, 1982), page unknown.

6.   LeBoeuf, *Working Smart*, p. 182.

7.   Denis Waitley, *Seeds of Greatness* (Old Tappan, NJ: Fleming H. Revell Company, 1983), p. 95.

8.   Gigi Tchividjian, *In Search of Serenity* (Portland, OR: Multnomah, 1990).

Chapter 19—A Heart That Shows It Cares

1.   Elisabeth Elliot, *Through Gates of Splendor* (Old Tappan, NJ: Fleming H. Revell Company, 1957), page unknown.

2.   Anne Ortlund, *The Disciplines of the Beautiful Woman* (Waco, TX: Word, Inc., 1977), p. 35.

3.   J. Sidlow Baxter, "Will and Emotions," *Alliance Life Magazine* (formerly Alliance Witness), November 1970. Used by permission. ·

4. Elizabeth George, *Woman of Excellence* (Christian Development Ministries, P.O. Box 33166, Granada Hills, CA 91394, 1987).

Chapter 20—A Heart That Encourages
1. Charles Caldwell Ryrie, *Balancing the Christian Life* (Chicago: Moody Press, 1969), pp. 96-97.
2. Ibid.
3. C.A. Stoddards, source unknown.

Chapter 21—A Heart That Seeks First Things First
1. Janice Ericson. Used by permission
2. Michael DeBoeuf, *Working Smart* (New York: Warner Books, 1979), pp. 129, 249.
3. *The Amplified Bible* (Grand Rapids, MI: Zondervan Bible Publishers, 1965), p. 302.
4. Pat King, *How Do You Find the Time?* (Edmonds, WA: Aglow Publications, 1975), page unknown.
5. Ibid.

Chapter 22—Following After God's Heart
1. Elizabeth George, *Loving God with All Your Mind* (Eugene, OR: Harvest House Publishers, 1994).
2. Edith Schaeffer, *Common Sense Christian Living* (Nashville: Thomas Nelson Publishers, 1983), p. 196.

Chapter 23—The Legacy of *A Woman After God's Own Heart*
1. Jim George, *A Man After God's Own Heart* (Eugene, OR: Harvest House Publishers, 2002).

Personal Notes

Personal Notes

Personal Notes

Personal Notes

Personal Notes

Personal Notes

Personal Notes

Personal Notes

Personal Notes

About the Author

Elizabeth George is a bestselling author who has more than four million books in print. She is a popular speaker at Christian women's events. Her passion is to teach the Bible in a way that changes women's lives. For information about Elizabeth's speaking ministry, to sign up for her mailings, or to purchase her books visit her website:

www.ElizabethGeorge.com

If you've benefited from *A Woman After God's Own Heart®*, you'll want the complementary book

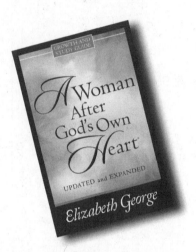

A
Woman After God's Own Heart®

**Growth
and
Study Guide**

This guide offers thought-provoking questions, reflective studies, and personal applications that will enrich your life as you study to become a woman after God's own heart.

This growth and study guide is perfect for both personal and group use.

A Woman After God's Own Heart® Growth and Study Guide
is available at your local Christian bookstore
or can be ordered from:

Elizabeth George
PO Box 2879
Belfair, WA 98528
1-800-542-4611
www.ElizabethGeorge.com

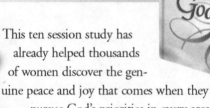

After God's Own Heart

Elizabeth George's *A Woman After God's Own Heart*® showed you how to draw closer to God, to your husband, to your family, and to become more effective in your work and ministry. These other bestselling books by Elizabeth and her husband, Jim, will help you and your family experience God's love and provision in greater measure and enable you to reach out to others with the hope and love of the gospel.

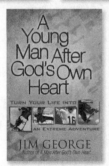
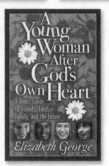

Order from
www.ElizabethGeorge.com
or available at bookstores everywhere!
Read sample chapters at www.harvesthousepublishers.com

BIBLE STUDIES *for*

BUSY WOMEN

Character Studies

Old Testament Studies

New Testament Studies

A WOMAN AFTER GOD'S OWN HEART® BIBLE STUDIES

*E*lizabeth takes women step-by-step through the Scriptures, sharing wisdom she's gleaned from more than 30 years as a women's Bible teacher.

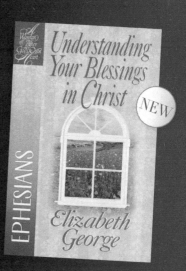

Books by Elizabeth George

- Beautiful in God's Eyes
- Finding God's Path Through Your Trials
- Following God with All Your Heart
- Life Management for Busy Women
- Loving God with All Your Mind
- A Mom After God's Own Heart
- The Remarkable Women of the Bible
- Small Changes for a Better Life
- Walking with the Women of the Bible
- A Wife After God's Own Heart
- A Woman After God's Own Heart®
- A Woman After God's Own Heart® Deluxe Edition
- A Woman After God's Own Heart®—A Daily Devotional
- A Woman After God's Own Heart® Collection
- A Woman's Call to Prayer
- A Woman's High Calling
- A Woman's Walk with God
- A Young Woman After God's Own Heart
- A Young Woman After God's Own Heart—A Devotional
- A Young Woman's Call to Prayer
- A Young Woman's Walk with God

Study Guides

- Beautiful in God's Eyes Growth & Study Guide
- Finding God's Path Through Your Trials Growth & Study Guide
- Following God with All Your Heart Growth & Study Guide
- Life Management for Busy Women Growth & Study Guide
- Loving God with All Your Mind Growth & Study Guide
- A Mom After God's Own Heart Growth & Study Guide
- The Remarkable Women of the Bible Growth & Study Guide
- Small Changes for a Better Life Growth & Study Guide
- A Wife After God's Own Heart Growth & Study Guide
- A Woman After God's Own Heart® Growth & Study Guide
- A Woman's Call to Prayer Growth & Study Guide
- A Woman's High Calling Growth & Study Guide
- A Woman's Walk with God Growth & Study Guide

Children's Books

- God's Wisdom for Little Girls
- A Little Girl After God's Own Heart

Books by Jim & Elizabeth George

- God Loves His Precious Children
- God's Wisdom for Little Boys
- A Little Boy After God's Own Heart

Books by Jim George

- The Bare Bones Bible® Handbook
- The Bare Bones Bible® Handbook for Teens
- The Bare Bones Bible® Bios
- A Husband After God's Own Heart
- A Man After God's Own Heart
- The Remarkable Prayers of the Bible
- A Young Man After God's Own Heart